SONG OF SAMADHI

MY EXPERIENCE WITH SUPER CONSCIOUSNESS

BIBHUTI BHUSAN MOHANTY

Contents

Foreword

Since the inception of life in mother's womb, and being born into this world, playing various roles till ascension unto the funeral pyre, all actions of us all, good or bad, right or wrong, proceed from three inherent desires:

1. Life/existence : No one wants to die. King & beggar, the weak & the strong, rich & poor alike, all fear death. Even an ant, when touched, runs away for fear of death. So, if we think carefully, it'll be seen that, all our actions are fundamentally in defence of existence!!

2. Knowledge/awareness : Whatever we see, hear or perceive through sense instruments we refer it to our memory and get the 'knowledge' of it. For example, we see a four legged shiny black docile living being walking & bleating in a particular manner and our memory reports it to us as a goat. Thus we 'know' it and we're satisfied. Now, suppose we come across a queer seven legged living being of say, unusual size and symmetry giving unusual sound, then ? We'll anxiously run from pillar to post to 'know' it. It'll be the talk of the town, with everyone crowding around helplessly and we'll not sit in peace. This is intrinsic in everyone. Why ?

3. Bliss/Joy/Happiness : The third aspect is, no one wants to be sorrowful. Who welcomes grief? Everyone, from amoeba to human race, runs hither and thither in fear of sorrow and search of happiness. Most of us take so much 'pain' running after selfish external sensual pleasure mongering, thinking that, it'll give us happiness. But Alas! This pursuit has opened the floodgates of despair, worries & sorrows before even we've hardly tasted the pleasure! But, the rocky thorny path of pleasure-seeking continues in hit and trial. Old men know it better.

And then, despite all our efforts, all of us are going to die!! No effort, no food, no medicine, no science can save our youthful vigour. Old age must cripple our body and senses. And disease can visit us anytime to cripple us even before old age!!

Ohh! The agony of struggle for life, for a morsel of food, for a moment of smile in hours of acute pain ! When, life throws life-threatening blows at us, when all our might and money are of no avail, when the frail frame of bones struggles to even crawl, the ego in us faces an adamantine wall that he just can't scale and looks up in despair. The exhausted and exasperated person seeks help from some super powerful entity. **And thus begins the quest for life here and hereafter.**

All the schools of religious beliefs, creeds and dogmas and the rest have sprung from this quest in hours of despair. Is there no way out then? Will all our coveted pleasure gardens and collections will end in smoke? Will our beautifully decorated body rot away, burn away, go into the mouth of jackals and vultures!!

Does God really exist? Will he solve my problems of disease and death, despair and despondency that no power on earth could solve? Will I ever get uninterrupted joy that will not be elusive? Can I get rid of this beggar's life and get rid of death once and for all!

Burdened with struggles and sorrows since childhood, my friend and classmate from REC (now NIT) Rourkela and author of this book Mr. Bibhuti Mohanty also got restless with these questions. But he didn't nibble at it. During college days, he'd slip into nearby hillside at dusk and spend hours in deep contemplation on these questions. He even attempted to flee from the campus for the Himalayas. But destiny brought him back. But his tryst with inner struggle went on, till, after three decades of inner struggle in blinding darkness and pathlessness, the truth flashed forth!! In an extraordinarily conscious state of mind, he realised, he felt, he saw, he directly and undeniably experienced, in a much more intense sense than we experience things in this world, that, what we call, God or Divinity or Sachidananda (Existence-Knowledge-Bliss absolute), Atma or Paramatma does exist. Not only does He exist, but also He is in the inmost of our very being. That which we had been searching in temples and churches, in mosques and Gurudwaras is intimately ever present within us!!

Out of acute compassion towards all human beings, to share his direct experience of the state of **realisation (**called **Samadhi in** Sanatana school of thinking) for the sincere strugglers after deathless life and unebbing Joy, upon my insistence put to words his own inexpressible moments and exalted state of coming face to face with the all pervading 'Atma' or Paramatma or God.

If this book kindles interest in a single reader in the quest for solving the mystery of death, disease, sorrows and unsurmountable struggles of this earthly life, this book will be a success.

Namaste at the Lotus feet of the loving Lord, the ocean of forgiveness !!

Er. Nirakara Satapathy

This book is one of a kind record of an arduous journey to the unseen truth. It lays a very broad framework of spirituality beyond different schools of thoughts or philosophies! It is spoken from an exalted state of consciousness. The magical spells are expressed as is, as various short poems in the "Song of Samadhi" chapter. The tone is grave as the subject is so. Transcending death is not a story. It is the culmination of an age old struggle for liberation. As chapter by chapter unfolds the mysteries of creation, the reader is transported to an inner world of solitude and joy. It is not based on a particular school of thought as truth is beyond all and one.

Sufferings and agonies is common to all from animals to humans. Some naively accept it as destiny, some try to avoid it by drugs and other habbits, while a rare few try to go to the root of it. And, out of many aspirants from many worlds a rare one somewhere sees the glorious Atman in full in first person. Time and space get overshadowed as the background substratum behind this mysterious cosmos is seen. On realization, the master magician is in sight playing with infinite number of creations with ease, all caught in the divine camera! The ambience turns nectarine as whole cosmos appears as a live dream land. One is wide awake and whole nature dances in adoration! And, in an inebriated and exalted state of consciousness the same helpless Jiva dances in ecstasy "Shivoham! Shivoham!". Salute to the Atman!!

When asked what is so special about realization which we experience in deep sleep and can experience using various drugs and intoxicants he says, "Oh no! Unmatchable indeed is the sweetness of Nirvikalpa. Neither the pleasure gardens of the highest heavens nor any intoxicant known so far, nor any relationship between man and woman can even faintly match the indescribable nectar. Even one drop is remembered for decades. Whole nature is poor to provide this rapture. Million fully boomed moons can't match its sweetness. The sweetness is real not any magic or metaphor. It satiates the unquenchable thirst of ego for ever. Ego after tasting it goes mad in ecstasy. Eternal spring returns, eternal existence returns, eternal love returns, eternal joy returns. Drunk and absorbed dances the ego almost externally unconscious even when out of the spell of Nirvikalpa. The pleasure hangover lingers for life and ego has no chance to stage a come back. Paradoxically, same ego plans its own destruction. Such is the value of Realization".

Let me briefly bring to you how the journey started during the author's college days with a sudden attempt to escape to the caves of the Himalayas. It is quite normal for indian yogis to start their search in solitude in the snow clad mountain peaks of the great Himalayas.

The All India Radio brought the shocking news "Bibhuti with so and so height and color is missing from the hostel of NIT Rourkela since...". It was 7th december 1987. The day was very cold and windy. We never imagined the "Persons Missing" news section would pour out the cruel words with so much precision. There was no room to disbileve it.

Our little world fell like a deck of cards. Our only hope to come out of chill penury came crashing. There was grave silence and heart rending cries in all corners of our little house. The young ones were wondering what the issue was. The news couldn't be kept hidden long and neighbors thronged our house and the atmosphere was sombre. All faces were pale pretending as if nothing had happened. The situation was nothing short of an occasion of death. With tear and a deep sigh I boarded the next available bus to his hostel some hundreds miles away. Last journey along the same road was so joyous, a sharp contrast to this one filled with sorrows. Last time, just a few months back in monsoon, filled with tons of dreams, along the same road flanked by lushgreen forest we had travelled for his admission. This is life.

Things were falling apart, prayer being the only option. Long discussions with hostel superindent and other friends of his yeilded no result. There was no clue as to where actually he had gone. With a heavy heart I returned home with no words to console my family.

A few days later, when all hope had departed, to our utter surprise, we saw the frail missing person at our door steps after a futile attempt to escape to the Himalayas in search of God.

This book is a record of his journey to eternity. It was a rare privilege to closely discuss with him the "Call of the Atman". I rarely believed his words. But, as I recall it was a dream come true after years of fierce struggle. I had the rare oppertunity to see the progress of his journey for truth from very close. I have seen the stormy days after his escapes. He tried one more time afterwards. Realization is the biggest treasure everybody is after. Now , as I see him engrossed and absorbed in meditation I realize what really meditation is, what really search is. I am still a novice in this pathless path.

I recall how passionately he sought the unseen inspite of dozens of obstacles. I wonder how he balanced his job with his noble ambition. We hardly could dissuade him from his path. With great determination he inched step by step to the climax of sadhana. Hope this little book serves as a little lamp for the struggling millions. I see the infinite flashing on his face. Still can't believe that the storm of liberation so rare to find was brewing well under our roof. The chapter on Samadhi is rare record of the ascent and descent. Realization is rare. And engaging with the person undergoing it from close quarters is rarer. Best wishes to all the readers!

Dr. Shashi Bhusan Mohanty

Preface

Who says Atman doesn't see? Who else has power to really see? Who says prayer doesn't connect? Who says sufferings can't end? As night falls and darkness envelops, a loud scream from a frightened kid immediately reaches mother. She hurries back calling "Don't fear; I am around. Leave the sand houses. They remain where they are. Can I ever be without you? You forgot, not me". We fear darkness yet won't leave it! Our prayer brings grace. Our prayer carries forward across lives. **Note:** "seeing" and "gracing" is neither mental nor physical. It is through God and Maya.

Maya deludes ego, while Atman or Brahman is ever free. Atman is beyond subject, object and perception. Atman doesn't partake in transactional activities of creations. Through Maya and God, Atman controls and witnesses' creation, while itself remaining detached. Cosmos is painted and repainted through power of Maya. It is individual self that transmigrates propelled by desire. Unless until Maya lifts by intense Vairagya or Bhakti or Nishkama Karma, truth remains a mystery. Our journey is from darkness to light; Our journey is from fear to freedom. Each one counts; each one is eternal! Sufferings is not in our fate; We are beyond both sufferings and fate. We are immortal.

Direct realization in a nutshell

Clearly seeing, experiencing, and identifying **infinite space** as the **indivisible and formless inner state** ofcosmos, signals realization. Expanded ego or infinitely conscious sees this state. The changing and illusive physical surroundings around a little body are **carved or projected** out from infinite space, just as idols are carved out from a massive rock. Infinite space is unchanging and seen with eye of wisdom as Maya lifts! In infinite space physical cosmos is painted. **"Seeing this Painting"** is seeing things as they really are. Whole cosmos both inner and outer (painting) is seen as swimming in Me (Seer). The infinite pull threatens the centre (little body in outer) to the extent of removing!!

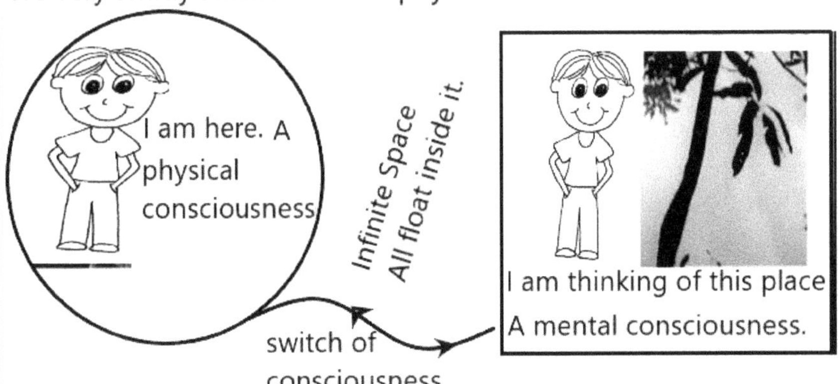

This infinite space further expands to SAT(pure infinite consciousness orSat-Chit-Ananda   or   Atman   or   Brahman   or   Nectar)   **in Nirvikalpa**!Conversely, SAT first contracts or condenses to ASAT (infinite space) as "first creation or seen". Infinite consciousness expands to SAT **in** Nirvikalpa! Conversely, SAT contracts to ASAT (infinite consciousness) as "first seer" of "first seen". Convergence between seer and seen is union with no distance or thought. Divergence is cosmic darkness or cosmos. All secondary or false seers or little egos along with their little false forms are carved out later from "first seer" and "first creation". Divergence between secondary seer and secondary seen is huge.

Hold your breath! Whole cosmos even when folded several times is not enough to fill even a point!! Can million shadows packed together fill even a dot? Also, there is nothing called 'time' as such If we don't recall; You are face to face with illusion in broad day light! Before realization, this world was separate lying outside the body; After realization this world is seen inside; Whether inside or outside, it comes into existence only when recalled!

Mukti:
> Pilgrimage is ending, Pilgrim is absorbed, world and mind both folded.
> World a sweet memory, a dream whether within or without.
> Still this shadow (body) hovers here (cosmos) for a while.
> Still this shadow returns here, pines over its dolls (relations) for a while.
> Separated is reconnected; Maya fashioned the illusion.
> Directions irrelevant in Infinite; All markers gone.
> That pull overshadows this.
> Periphery leaving its centre (body); Things no more are to hold it back.

Decades ago, during early pre-university days in Puri, I've spent evenings after evenings in your temple precincts, but, lost in the load of my own world, I never saw you in the temple!

This is neither any scriptural interpretation or belief nor any philosophical imagination. It's revealed beyond all doubts in the hours of coming face to face with Reality. It's infinitely more clinching evidence than the outcomes of scientific laboratory tests!

Yes, God is there, Atman is there, all pervading blissful nectarine Divinity is there; And take heart, He can be attained by each one of us if we call out with self-belief and march on in the right earnest!

The two birds' metaphor from Mandukya Upanishad depicts how we are trapped by our own actions helplessly wheeling the cycle of birth and death. Thick cloud of Maya envelops the lower bird.

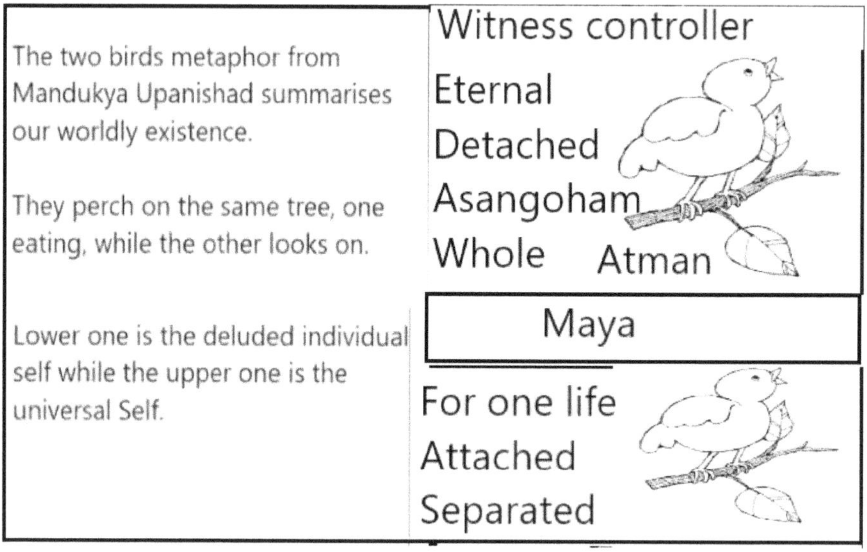
The two birds metaphor from Mandukya Upanishad summarises our worldly existence.
They perch on the same tree, one eating, while the other looks on.
Lower one is the deluded individual self while the upper one is the universal Self.
Witness controller
Eternal
Detached
Asangoham
Whole
Atman
Maya
For one life
Attached
Separated

Ages pass in fear in valleys of death. Sufferings look unending. Nothing seems to work till search goes deep. Burdened and frightened of one more graveyard the lower bird cries, goes inconsolable, seeks truth alone and holds back from grabbing the morsels thrown at it.

Ego holds back;   No more get carried by the stream of emotions fed by senses; A great split starts among the antahkarana;   Pratyahara that looked so tough begins. Mind comes under scanner!

Ego takes a different road the eternal road of truth and solitude; The perennial Atman absorbs it;   The dance of liberation begins;   The nectarine merger starts in the eternal sky of ecstasy and rapture; The witnessing begins. Death fear lifts for ever.

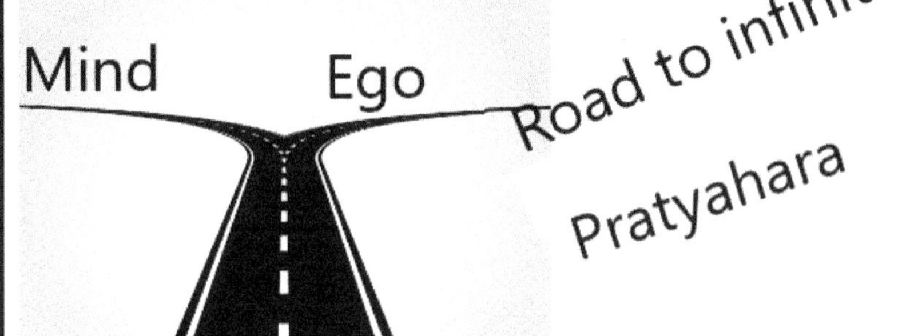

It glances the upper bird and falls in love. Intimacy rises. It remains intensely absorbed. As absorption rises, same world that looked so real and invincible is seen as a dream land. It recalls.

What am I doing here with this monkey (mind)?
What are they (senses) offering me?
Why am I fearing for shadows ?

Reflect and see what this 'seeing' is.

Why am   I jumping (rebirth) from branch
to branch, pining, lamenting, bleeding over
trifles;

Its image moves, it doesn't; Its image subject to time, it is not;
Its image does,   it doesn't; Its image thinks, it doesn't;
Its image eats,   it doesn't; It is detached.
Its image dies,   it doesn't;   Asangoham! Asangoham!

All things around us are projections of memory through mind. Individual memory is superposed on universal memory. For seekers on earth, universal **memory** is realized at a very advanced stage, and only after that, poor ego sees the mesmerizing creation in full. A wonder phase of life called **'Aware Living'** starts. Firmament is ablaze and ego dances in ecstasy and rapture. Tear comes to eyes in utter disbelief. The thief (ego) is within the infinite mines of love. Not a handful, not a bagful, its gold raining all over. Immortal strikes back. Ego is disarmed without a finger raised. Who has power to remain unmelt in the current of infinite love. Yes, it's the entry in the inner **space of the Atman**. The soaring divine emotions is too difficult to resist. Tear keeps flowing. It was suppressed for ages. Destiny is in sight. At times, without any worldly reason, same ego cries the cry of freedom. Atman has returned, eternal companion is back. Life is full.

The very witness and controller it so often discussed unaware has held it in deep embrace. Earth and sky have met in joy. Eternal spring of liberation is everywhere. Million fount heads of bliss are seen in action. **This signals realization**.

Senses and mind dance nonstop inebriated, never ever used to this kind of abundance. Unfulfilled dreams long cherished and forgotten in despair come true. All happen now, this very moment around it. Ego is right in the helm of affairs; It is thrust into the limelight it so much hankered after for ages. Paradoxically, neither anybody is left to shower praise, nor it has any interest left in getting praised; All perceptions about this cosmos changed in a glance. This is no ordinary light but, the light of the Atman. The union has begun. The temple of love is no more dimly lit. Million fully bloomed moons can't match the brilliance of his glaze. Brahmajyoti has engulfed the myriad brahmandas.

The beggar ego has embraced the idol and idol is speaking to it. "Come, why away? Come a little closer. Let me heal your wounds in the long journey. Come, only you and me nobody in between. Let heavens go to hell". It still can't believe, first dismissing it as a passing dream. The heavenly spell overshadows all. Withdrawal is total. Traveller is absorbed, subject is lost. And divine talks to divine. Gradually ascent to samadhi is effortless. It realizes it is well past the highest heavens, call it Vaikuntha, call it Gopa Loka or by any other words, result is same, indescribable, and absorbing.

It is at last close to all the revealing climax in the cosmic theatre of Maya. It recalls how it took recourse to intoxicant, liquor and what not for a little warmth and joy. What love after all it got after so much struggle? How long the earthly unions last? In a few seasons love fades, relationship turns a burden. From where material things can satiate ego's infinite thirst? Although forgotten, ego is after all 'That' in disguise and what on heavens can please it in full?

Now, it recalls in shame its ugly fights over trifles, not aware it was the magician in its own magical world with its magical wand lost in excessive greed. As cage opens, same ego waits a while in wonder!

> Fort open; Cage open; Still the wonderstruck waits for a while adoring the images.
>
> Now as a free bird it looks at the little cup, the grains it grabbed in hunger, the little water, and the iron chain...
>
> It looks at the dolls (shadow like own body and bodies of relations) it played with for ages. Separation from shadows is a sweet pain.

Once maya lifts and realization starts, any spell of worldly pleasure pulls ego afar to the hinterland of samadhi. Withdrawal from mind and senses happens effortlessly by hanging a little carrot before them. Ego stays dipped in ecstasy.

Note: Ego is beyond five koshas and the gatherer and integrator of senses and mind. 'Split' below is an apparent separation from the infinite through Maya. A stray stream of consciousness flows unaware of the infinite. 'Merger' means the stray stream sees the infinite and attempts to unite.

Oh mind! Oh senses!
Don't stop me today.
Let me drink a little more,
Let me see a little more,
Let me be in his embrace a little.
Oh mind! Oh senses!
We have shared for ages in nest after nest,
Today my beloved returns long after our split,
Don't come in the way today.
Oh mind! Oh senses!
You threatened enough, you frightened enough,
It is time to part ways,
Now stay away, his fever is rising here there everywhere.

Split and Merger

You threw morsels at me,
Now me throwing back at you.
Hold this little music, hold this little sight
Let me go.

Object Meditation

Drowning the subject too.

Ego repents and laments. It realizes who really is behind this creation. It realizes it is neither body nor mind. It recognizes the real Self the oneself of all. Its desire for material things wanes.

Neither the shape nor the one behind it nor the surrounding can stand apart from real Self.

As the one behind recalls infinite space, it forgets both shape and surrounding,

The one behind body is our ego or false self. In intense pain and helplessness, ego prays for freedom, unaware of what this cosmos really is, what truth really is and where the path to liberation is. Each prayer in tear is a faint recall, a little connect to the whole. As prayer to the unknown gathers force, faith returns, hope returns, rhythm returns in the otherwise chaotic life. And, when time is ripe, destiny no more remains destiny. The magical spell cast by Maya gets dispelled. And Jiva outwits the star and enters the exquisite and celestial state of existence beyond all heavens.

One as infinite consciousness sees the mystical infinite space that defied the sight for ages. One in utter surprise beholds cosmos as a gigantic shadow swimming inside it, all ferocity gone, all laws tamed. The tune turns sublime. The dance of liberation begins.

As Jiva tastes infinite, existence turns eternal, whole cosmos is seen within. Closer still, "I am cosmos both inner and outer" as "in-ness" too goes in Nirvikalpa. The cosmos that appeared external and separated from ego's little body is seen spread inside. The little ego that appeared separated from other egos expands infinitely. This two-fold **expansion signals realization**. It is **Savikalpa** as a faint view of cosmos is still perceivable. What a sublime view!

Pure infinite Consciousness is Atman which is realized through subsequent **Nirvikalpa** as experiencer dissolves. All thoughts (illusive paints) go fainter and fainter till all internal and external consciousness go eternal. And this "going eternal" is "entering Nirvikalpa". This mesmerizing innermost expansion is awe-inspiring. No seer, no seen, no seeing, only truth is as is. The triad collapses. Savikalpa is a path breaking revelation.

No space photo is required for peeping into creation. No space photo can show the inner state of cosmos. An attempt is made to bring this rare experience although million books can't put the sublime experience. Nirvikalpa is not an experience, thus no definition is possible. "Neti, Neti" can be a hint.

Two-fold and simultaneous expansion mentioned above is faintly put here. Salute to the Atman!

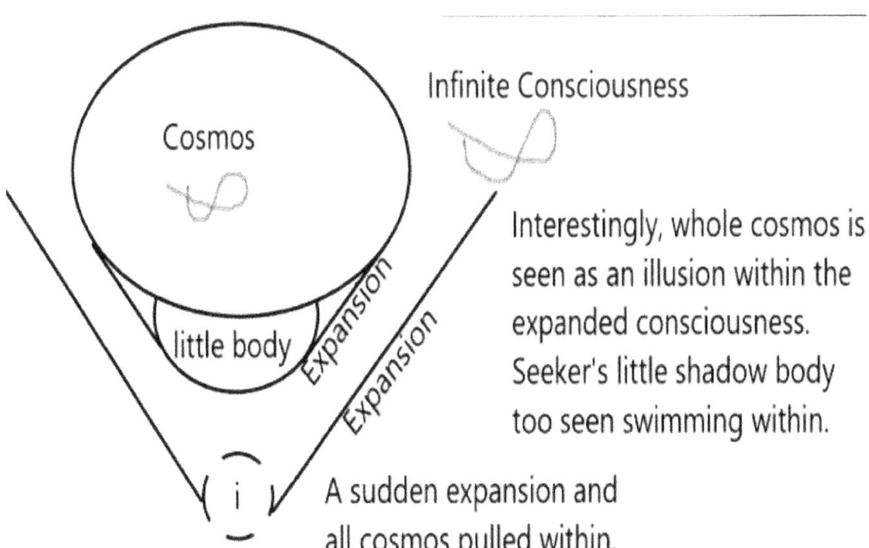

As cloud of ignorance disperses in the light of wisdom, world turns a dream land. Like actions in a movie, all worldly actions are seen among shadows. Seeker no longer mistakenly takes a rope as a snake in darkness. The liberated goes beyond the law of karma. **Infinite absorbs the finite**.

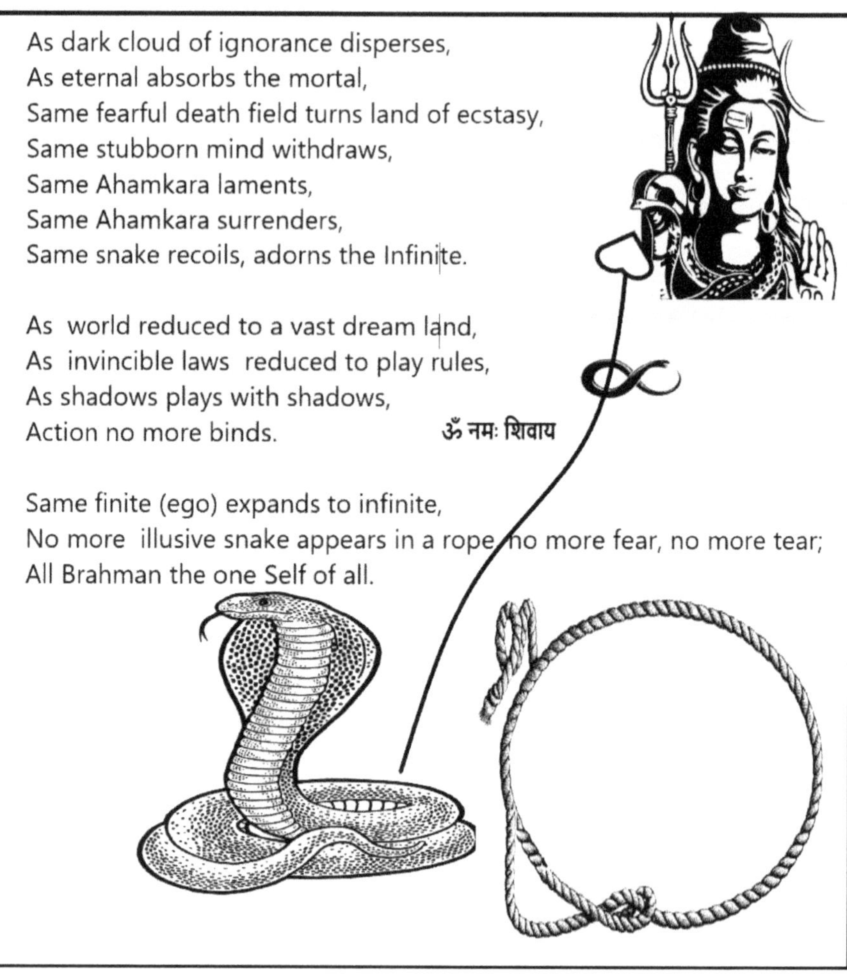

As dark cloud of ignorance disperses,
As eternal absorbs the mortal,
Same fearful death field turns land of ecstasy,
Same stubborn mind withdraws,
Same Ahamkara laments,
Same Ahamkara surrenders,
Same snake recoils, adorns the Infinite.

As world reduced to a vast dream land,
As invincible laws reduced to play rules,
As shadows plays with shadows,
Action no more binds.

Same finite (ego) expands to infinite,
No more illusive snake appears in a rope, no more fear, no more tear;
All Brahman the one Self of all.

Ages after,
As Jiva recalls in tear,
Spell cast by her dispelled,
Eternal spring flows,
This magic begins to set in that.
Cage breaks, bird infinitely aware,
Wonderstruck waits a while recalling stays here,
In fear and worry hardly saw it in full,
Breeze of liberation intoxicates,

Departure moment draws closer,
Jivatma outgrows cosmos,
Dance of union starts in internal sky of joy.

Intent of this effort is to affirm that Atman has eternal existence, and we can recognize that as clearly as we recognize things of this material world. This provides hope and strength to the solitary traveller in the pathless path for truth. This is a record of live samadhi for benefit of whole creation.

Atman or Brahman or pure infinite consciousness is the nectarine and eternally existent reality without a second. When time is ripe, the seeker dying for liberation realizes this very cosmos as an illusion. I-consciousness born of apparent association of infinite consciousness to body-mind-intellect is limited, deluded and changes from birth to birth as body-mind-attribute changes. Atman is beyond mind, body, and delusion. Atman is beyond subject, object and perception. Atman is omnipotent, omniscient, and omnipresent. It is the false or apparent I-consciousness that takes rebirth as long as it is under the spell of Maya. I-consciousness is the false enjoyer of the false fruit of action in the false world of illusion. Causal layer of this instance of creation is created through the illusive power of Maya.

Through Maya individuation happens. And, moment to moment through mind and desire individual memory is materialized as physical body and surroundings along the trail of attention. World is a dream. World rises and sets in mind from memory. In attention, rises the things and in absence of attention the things disappear in memory. I-consciousness rises as long as worldly things are accepted as real and desire to enjoy them exists.

In "Aham Brahmasmi or I am Brahman", Aham refers to the real Self. I-consciousness is identification only with a tiny part of creation (body) and seeing the rest as separate. I-consciousness rises as a narrow and apparent association of infinite with finite. The stronger the association, the stronger the ego. As Maya lifts and same Jagat perceived as illusive, the bondage of finite to the cage of name and form breaks. With own will the infinite expands to Maya, and through Maya creates Jiva and enters in Jiva as Jivatma or ego. The dissociation of I-consciousness from body allows the I-consciousness to expand infinitely till 'I' is completely lost in the flood of bliss. Million flood gates of infinite love devour the hungry ego during ascent to Samadhi or realization. The ego expands to infinite consciousness as the infinitely conscious sees the whole world floating within. Further ahead in Nirvikalpa, the infinitely conscious goes totally drunk and unconscious to the external world. "Shivoham! Shivoham!" dances the same helpless Jiva in ecstasy. This is the internal conquest after Maya is vanquished.

In Me the whole, whole nature rises and floats,
Ever intoxicating if part is aware of whole,
Parted and separated it (Jiva) cries in pain,
Deluded in darkness circles the wheel of death,
In Me the stage, drama, actors, and audience,
In Me sets the cosmos.

From the mesmerizing viewpoint of infinite, objects look strange, massless, and illusive shapes. The boundary of physical vision limited by power of physical eye breaks. The boundary of mental vision limited by power of mental eye too breaks. Finite consciousness expands to infinite consciousness. Infinite consciousness condenses to infinite space and all cosmoses seen flowing within just as clouds are seen flowing within sky. Clearer the view of infinite space, the fainter the things. One is in alien land. All relations and friends look shadow like. Who remains to do actions? An indivisible undifferentiated view of cosmos remains. All clocks stop. What past? What present? What future? One is in a dream world, wide awake.

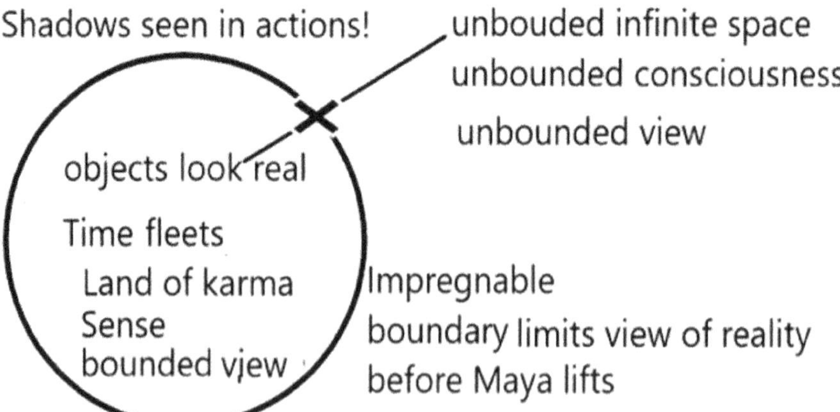

Maya fashions the world. Through the replication power of Maya, one Self of all appears to be many just as in dream we replicate into several dream characters. On wakeup from the world of Maya, seeker realizes "I was the creation. I was the Maya".

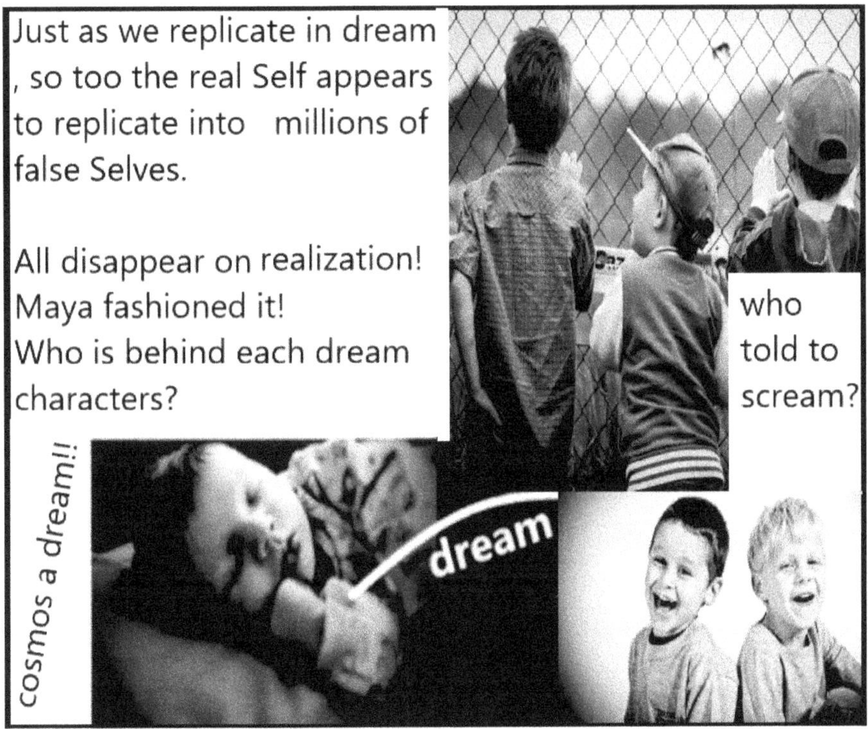

Ages after as Maya lifts, it is the same ego that expands infinitely till it is completely drowned. The drowning increases over a period as remaining desire is slowly overcome by the constant light of the Atman. I-consciousness is beyond the five koshas. I-consciousness recognizes and realizes the Atman without any need of introduction. As impurities of mind go, same I-consciousness shines. The merger of apparent I-consciousness in Atman is Samadhi. With every recall of Atman, I-consciousness disappears and with every recall of material things (under spell of maya), I-consciousness reappears. Mark the subtle yet fundamental difference between Ego (impure and limited I-consciousness) and Atman (pure and infinite consciousness). Attachment to illusive things is impurity which lifts as Maya lifts. Throughout the book wherever I-consciousness is mentioned, it should be understood in this context.

Destiny: Let us take a closer look at our regular life and understand our limitations.

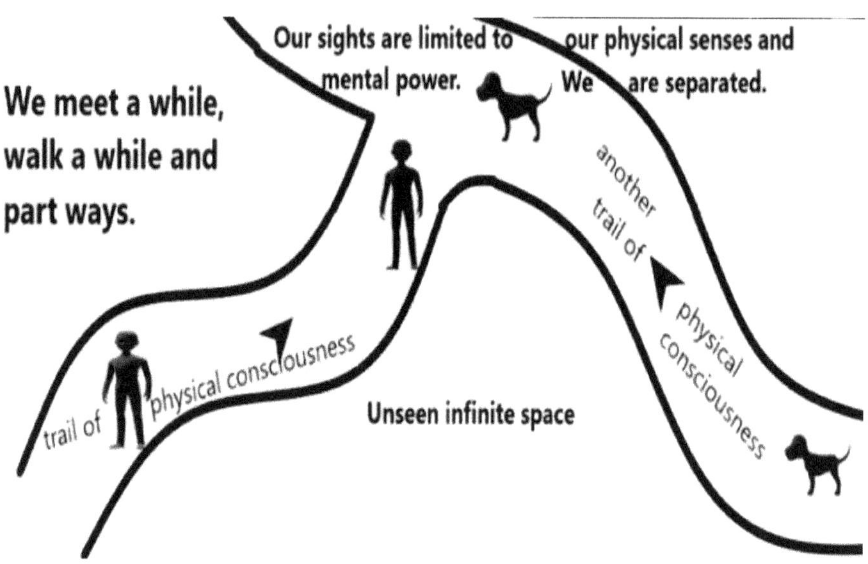

We are physically separated from the rest of nature through our individual bodies. Our views are limited. When by chance or deliberation we meet at worldly level, we engage a while unaware of what is happening elsewhere same very moment to rest of the world. Next, we part ways and engrossed with other thoughts forget the meet. Our journey continues unaware of 'where we appear from' and 'where eventually we head to'. When we walk on a road, we are unaware of what is happening to the rest of the world same moment as our views are confined to the limit of our physical senses. We think of faraway relations in mind little aware what is happening to them that very moment. We don't know what is in store for us next moment. We call our life the handiwork of destiny. Still, we talk tall, we promise a lot.

What big happens on realization?

With lifting of Maya, as Jiva lands in infinite space as infinite consciousness, the view of creation is simultaneous, parallel, and whole. Consciousness is millions of times faster than light. Jiva's mind no longer roams serially along a tiny trail of physical views unaware of the trails taken by others. Physical senses no longer confine the sight to a few things at a time unaware of what is happening to other things elsewhere at the same time. The experiences are path breaking.

All cosmoses are seen floating as massless images within one's infinitely expanded consciousness. Jubilation begins. Questions stop, blaming fate stops. Who else left to blame? All silenced. Million thunders can't distract anymore. This is Dharana.

The question **"Who am I?"** is answered in realization. This is the most important and most misinterpreted question of creation! After first glance of the Atman, one realizes what false self is and over a period all attachments drop till one is firmly established in Nirvikalpa.

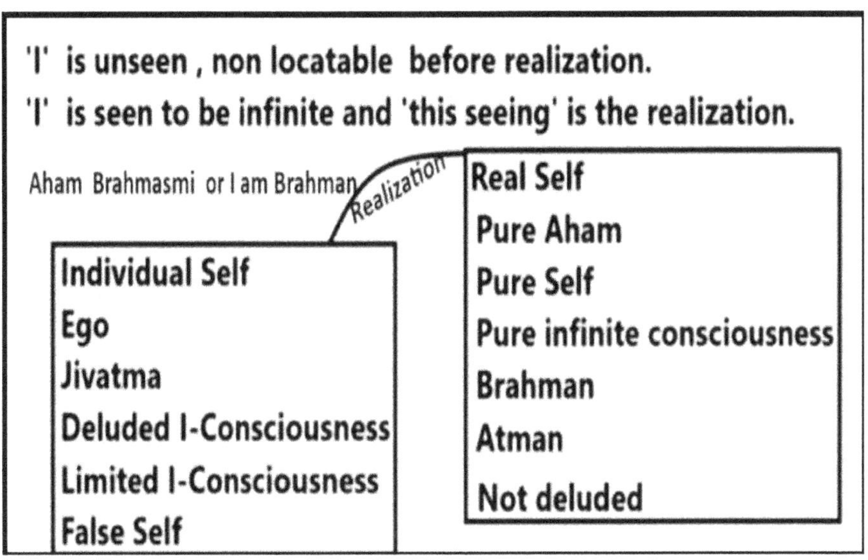

The real Self is pure infinite consciousness without any attributes and actions. The real Self is eternal without any desire and thought (Nirvikalpa), without any dirt (Niranjana), without any modification (Nirvikara), without any form, ever liberated (Nitya Mukta) and ever pure (Nirmala).

A very strange expansion and contraction is realized frequently. Rising and falling of I-consciousness is clearly experienced. One realizes the making and breaking of Me the false owner. One realizes how the body is grabbed and released. This is a critical observation.

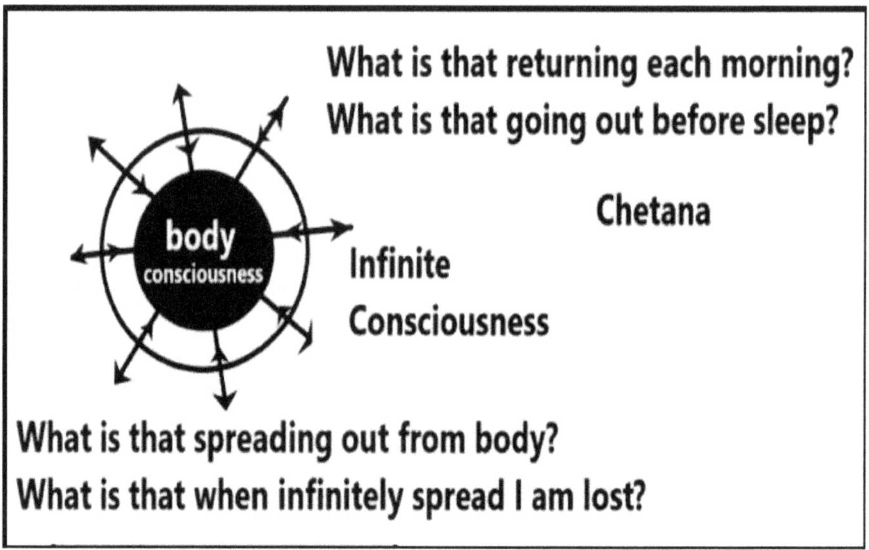

The rise of body consciousness as soon as mind builds shape, and the rise of ego as the owning consciousness remains a mystery for normal human beings. The fall of body consciousness as expansion starts and I-consciousness leaves the body is mesmerising. It solves the mystery of death and rebirth for ever. It is synonymous to something entering the house and leaving the house.

The celestial dance of liberation beyond all the heavens is between 'Nirakara + Akara' and 'Nirakara'. The process of '+ (association)' and '- (dissociation)' is the critical aspect of realization. It too is behind death and rebirth. Further discussion on it is out of the scope of this short book and may be clarified separately. "What is that spreading out?" is the bone of contention among many schools of spirituality. Whatever the terminology is, whoever has tasted it, has gone beyond mind and ego.

Atman is the canvas (substratum) of canvas (maya). Cosmos (images) is painted on Maya. Atman is detached. It is the false ego that dances in the infinite theatre of maya. As her spell is dispelled ego dances the dance of liberation.

Speech bounces from truth! Traveller is absorbed. Truth alone triumphs. Satyameva Jayate! All Illusions fall apart with the fall of the false centre (ego). Many have travelled. Many are travelling. Hope this little song of Samadhi helps all seekers a little in the direction of truth. Seeker must travel the path alone. Seeker must taste the immortal bliss alone. It is seeker's world, it is seeker's will, it is seeker's walk. Travel well oh traveller! Thou art that!

A very sweet Odia song "Re Aatman Nidra Parihari" comes to mind. It requests each Jiva to wake up from slumber, open the eye of mind and behold, how the life current is silently flowing with immense speed to meet the frightening waves roaring in the ocean of death. See, how in that current is washed away all the sukha (pleasures) whose memory keeps Jiva hooked to Samsara. See, how one misses the golden opportunity of human birth by lamenting over past. Wake up and run fast oh Jiva! Oh Jiva! seek Eshwar leaving this transient dream!

Vairagya slowly develops in misery. Pain is very difficult to bear. Nobody can take many of our deep-rooted pains barring a few surface ones. Pain comes uninvited just as pleasure. Who doesn't cry for youth in old age? Who loves wrinkles? Who doesn't cry for good health in diseased condition? Who doesn't want love and care when uncared and left out in the cruel race of samsara? Who does not fear death of own body and the close ones? How often we sob in private and carry on? These painful messages are all over cosmos and applicable to every being. Viveka cries out 'Mukti! Mukti!' when death hunts.

Lord buddha was a prince, yet he was worried. He knew the uncertainty of states of a being. In a moment all go, and quite often when wounded and hunted by time, whole world is incapable to protect. Sorrow is for vairagya to develop. Paradoxically, as one glimpses Atman, in one moment all pain go. Cosmos is a magic, a dream. As you think, so shall you become. Cosmos is just a thought. Think high, think immortality. There is nothing in what you see and hear around you in awake state, except the perceptions of the little mind. As ego expands, it turns universal encompassing Jagat. Ego is cornered at the end by own Viveka and it desperately cries for mukti and truth flashes. That truth is "Thou art that!".

Just before samadhi, mind is filled with extreme compassion, kind feelings for whole creation run riot and call for eternal freedom is loud and clear. One cries for whole creation, be it humans, be it animals. One prays for liberation of the whole world. World's sufferings become one's sufferings. One can't enjoy. All competitions stop. Who is the competitor to be defeated? Cries of creations from far and near trouble the mind. Mind shades its grossness, it goes sublime. One's sensitivity is sky high. One silently cries for whole creation. This phase is very close to samadhi.

We again and again tread the same perilous path and waste precious moments in wishful thinking's. All our thoughts in time and space are wishful, like lines on water, like shapes in mirage. Life current finishes moment by moment and we are enmeshed in the pursuit of happiness which will never be realized in this universe. Run for real life. When maya's forces would return to snatch this body away nobody knows. All lifeless images are playing among themselves. Nobody is ours. As body grows old and begs for morsels of love, it is refused. Wrinkles appear, death hunts all over. Same moon, same sun and same lightening dance in the beautiful cloud over the beautiful hill but, the eye is feeble, mind is worried to notice. Gloom is all over. They will burn the same beautiful body and come back. Same body is left to vultures and bacteria to feast on it. Same dust so quickly cleaned is the bed where the body decomposes.

Relentless fear for own and the dear ones chase the mortal in the dangerous valleys of desire. In some lives, desire remains strong with no means to fulfil and in hunger Jiva gasps for freedom from suffocation. Desire strangulates and chokes the Jiva in many lives in lower worlds where fight for survival is severe due to scarcity of resources. There are lives when intellect is very low to defend against odds of life. Creature is eaten raw while sleeping in the cave by other creatures in cold, dark, and hostile terrains.

How often we see a beggar moving from temple step to temple step in hunger, eyes on food and a little sleep. One is helpless and at the receiving end in many lives. All turn heads away in despise when the worms feast on the festering wounds. This is the path of samsara. Why don't you see? Freedom from this jail is the objective and tear, sob and crying show the path.

The beginning of samadhi and the terrible fight is briefly recorded here. In my case,the "real Self absorbing ego" is realized in middle age when dawn (early life) and afternoon (late youth) was passing after long wait for truth and gloom was looming all over.

Key to victory is keeping the sagging spirit up in the most daunting situations. Physical ailments force the attention on body. Mental turbulence in trying situations squeeze the hope and the little lamp of liberation is challenged again and again to the extent of total extinction. Darkness can only be eradicated by truth. Truth is still afar.

The little light of **viveka** is still very dim although sufficiently improved. Ocean of samsara is infested with giant and hungry sharks of subconscious desires. One's resolve for truth is seriously tested as never before, once viveka (discriminating intelligence) declares a passive (through ego) and indirect war against body, senses, and mind. Ego is now sufficiently weakened by fire of vairagya and guided by light of viveka. Viveka gains more ground with nod from ego. It is in centre stage although still passive as usual. The simmering discontent against desires brews into a war. Fierce fight with inner nature starts. This is the decisive battle and ego is flooded with grace as all divine forces corner the dark forces (desires) of maya, and the fort of mind is besieged and set ablaze at last! Ego laments, repents, and limps as it realizes the real Self. Ego holds back from mind and senses. Ego expands infinitely into infinite consciousness by dissociating from body. Probably, lord Buddha referred to this fight as the epic fight against the forces of mara.

As vairagya develops, the fight for woman and gold in the external world is nothing compared to the inner fight between viveka and intellect-mind-sense-ego. Whole world colludes to uproot the little delicate plant of viveka and there is every chance of failures lurking at the seeker from all sides. Whatever branch the seeker holds onto breaks. These are trying days in the journey to truth.

Cremation ground too is noisy and unsafe. Hopes fall apart one by one. Sadness deepens, gloom thickens, dark cloud of despair frightens. Friend's part ways. Relations turn head scorning and scoffing. At times, physical hunger is at height with no means to fulfil as the supply chain is long cut off by own hand. One is on the hardest road with no connectivity. Alms too is difficult to come by. Stick of faith is not yet strong enough to face the volley fired from angry haters and the onslaught of marauding creatures.

Ochre robe too is not safe as many hates, and stone pelting is not uncommon. Where to go tomorrow? Who would listen? The stone has not yet spoken. The idol is not yet live. Stick of faith is too brittle. The temple precinct too is not safe as many masked beggars threaten the feeble seeker. Where to go? Who would accept the fallen (in the coloured eyes of others)? Who will side? Who will be kind? Forest caves too become the preying ground as the emaciated traveller is too feeble to defend. Diseased, wounded and trembling with fear, one's hungry finger can't even reach the fruit. While climbing over the stiff slippery rocks in cold and dark night chased by tiger, one can hardly recall the unknown and unseen lord's name. While coming to the path of truth is difficult after ages of struggle with death, it is equally difficult to keep the hope of freedom alive. External and internal situations at times remain very unfavourable. This is the fight with the forces of maya. The king of kings is paraded for stealing morsels of illusive food and love from his own kingdom. The lonely I-consciousness is terribly challenged, the unfed senses are in revolt, the fort of mind too impregnable to break, the voice of freedom is not even a whisper. In excruciating pain and frustration, one often returns. This path of yoga is not easy. It is difficult to travel. The yogis walk cautiously in fear of fall. But the weather changes for better very soon.

Below little song attempts to describe my first absorption by the Atman (pure infinite consciousness). We all talk of 'I' but, never realize what really it is, where really it is. It defies all our intelligence. For the first time, we experience what 'I' really is in the blazing light of the Atman. Paradoxically, when 'I' is seen for the first time after ages, it is seen lamenting in its death bed, yearning for freedom from the clutches of body! Ego slips away to the depth of solitude in the background as Atman absorbs it, while body-mind-senses are still relishing the morsels of food in the foreground.

Waited and waited, counting moment after moment in deep despair;

Painfully saw morning turning afternoon, tired feet still unwilling to return

Deep solitude had prevailed everywhere;

All friends and relations had long parted;

Suddenly heard a call loud and clear, turned back to find no one;

Thought it was an illusion;

Again heard a soft call, a pleasant inner one, still pondered, who was it?

And saw someone capturing from within;

Deeply possesing me, pulling me from within; Who is He within me?

Is He the answer to my decade old question "Who am I?".

Now, when He comes, I am silent; When He stays I am different;

When He leaves I am disturbed!

The beginning of Samadhi

Salute to my Atman!
My beloved Krishna!

Who is He within me? Who is drawing me within?

A sweet and pleasant experience, a connection connecting me to cosmos;

A different intoxication, a different possession , never ever seen before;

Who is He coming and going tearing apart my little existence?

Who is He possessing me, thrilling me, landing me in a different dimension,
far away from space, time, and phenomena;

Who is He within me so sweet so liberating?O mind!, can't you see Him?

The whole living has undergone a sea change; The whole universe looks different
No in, no out, no up, no down, no there, no here.

Yes, someone is within; Yes, **He is my Atman my beloved my aradhya devata!**

Note: A kind of shyness overwhelms and me eagerly waits for Me;
A sweet companion, a sweet beloved, so tall to embrace in full, so tall
for the beggar. After a month or so all shyness gone; Merger deepens;
Yes, it is Samadhi!! i-stream expanding to infinite and contracting!

The expansion of ego to infinite and contraction back to ego is regularly experienced thereafter. Some constituent experiences noted down as is.

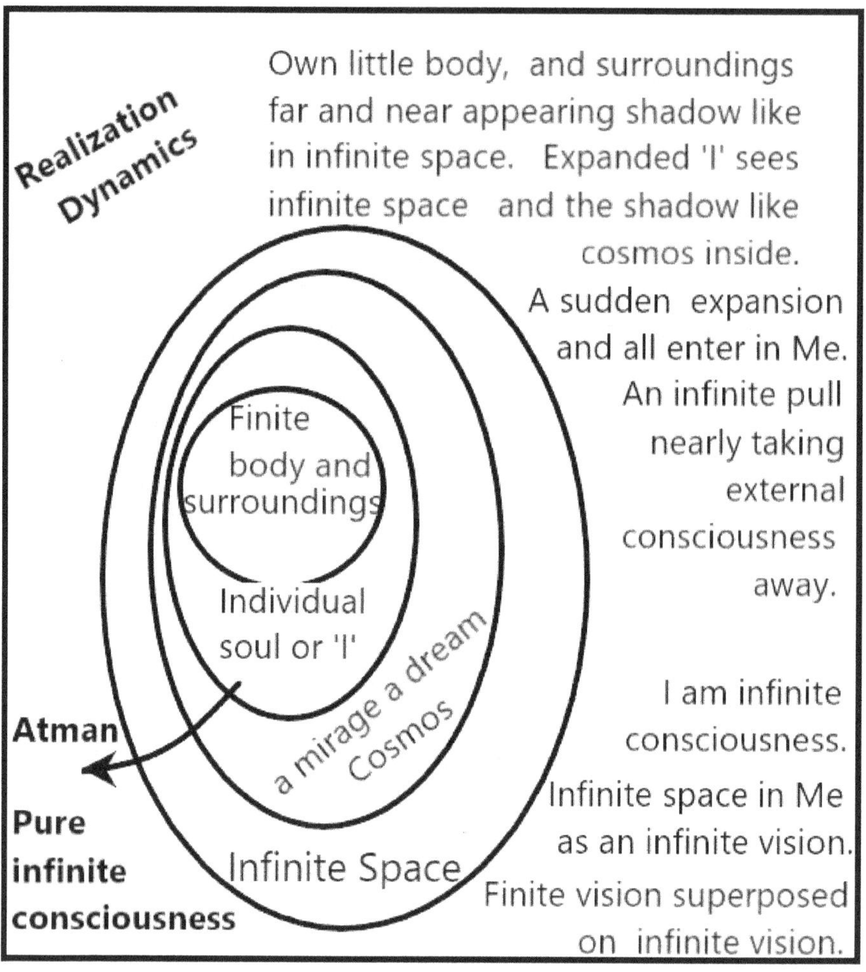

All cosmoses turn a mirage,
All cosmoses turn a dream.
Every morning it is pulled infinitely,
And all cosmoses devoured within.
Every night at sleep, it pulls back.

Every attempt to realize that is not a wastage of time. Rather, pursuit of truth should be the primary goal of all beings. The search for absolute freedom and the subconscious desire for eternal love spans across lives. Any unfinished effort in that direction in a life is an invaluable asset. All other assets are transient except the all-pervading Atman. Who told Atman doesn't exist? Atman alone is all else ephemerals. Atman is beautiful and just one glance is enough for lifelong intoxication. Atman is the intoxicant that really lifts the drooping spirit above the mundane thoughts, and the celestial union with the Atman overrides all other joys. Ego in just one glance gets disarmed. This very world we all complain of turns the eternal land of ecstasy and joy. One dances the dance of liberation wonderstruck and intoxicated. It realizes that it is neither the body nor the mind nor the little I-consciousness. It is the Atman the pure infinite consciousness ever complete, ever existent, ever blissful. It realizes whole cosmos is swimming within mind as a vast dream land. It no longer fears death. The ego in its death bed asks the beloved Atman "Oh Atman! Wait a while. Let me behold my dolls (relations and own little body) and sand houses a little more. Let me recall my numerous nests and relations spread across lives a little more. Worried, I failed to see your creation in full. In the departing hours they look awesome and profound oh Atman!".

And the mesmerizing union in the firmament of super consciousness thrills the same self-exiled prisoner. In the valleys of mind, it roamed in pain for morsels of food and love. It knocked this door, that door in pursuit of pleasure. All attempts were in vain. The door of the cage had looked unbreakable. In despair it had returned.

The famous quote of the **Buddha** flashes on the first Darshana of the priceless beloved.

The Light of Asia:
Many a house of life hath held me,
Seeking ever him who wrought these prisons of the senses,
Sorrow fraught, sore was my ceaseless strife!
But now, thou builder of this tabernacle - thou!
I know thee! Never shalt thou build again these walls of pain,
Nor raise the roof-tree of deceits, nor lay fresh rafters on the clay,
Broken thy house is, and the ridge-pole split!
Delusion fashioned it!
Safe pass i thence deliverance to obtain.

Sufferings if channelized helps lotus (sahasrara) to bloom and one floats in infinite space. All material worlds vanish or remains mirage like. No thirst, no fear, no thing remains; All nectar, all dream, all wonder of wonders. It takes years to come out of the awe, till one merge in Nirvikalpa for ever.

Following chapters seriously attempt to clear several of our deep rooted doubts like "If one is unconscious within samadhi, then who tells the indescribable?" , "How can creator tolerate its creation seething in pain? , "Is world real?" , "How one enters samadhi?" , "Is Atman real?" , "Is karma and rebirth true?" , "What happens during samadhi?", "Is nectar really the sweetest or a mere metaphor?".

The chapter on samadhi briefly puts the different revelations. One in samadhi intensely feels the tear of other seekers. One in samadhi has no jealousy or hatred for any creature in any corner of the creation and out of infinite compassion passes on as is the priceless message for the millions of seekers in tears spread across infinite number of worlds. The path to samadhi spans several lives and maya does lift in vairagya. As maya lifts, all principles behind phenomenal world unfold. *Whole cosmos turns a vast dream land in mind.*

Why we seek eternal life? Youth looks unending. Unending dreams keep the eyes coloured. The story of this life has just begun. The spring has just thrown its magical spells.

The smell of fresh flowers lifts the spirit. Success looks so easy. Romance is at its peak. In pride the head touches sky. Friends and relations look deep reliable and perennial. It takes the luxuries for granted. With great pride it conquers. Mind soars higher and higher touching sky. Full moon pulls the mind afar to the horizon of romance. Breeze of love flows from morning to night.

Tune of earthly union thrills. Life looks full and intoxicating. Hope is on rise. It feels science alone as the perfect tool for materialising its spiralling ambitions. All look rosy and within reach. Ambitions keep rising and promises look so easy to keep. Sunshine everywhere.

World looks real and full. All Engagements are intense. It hardly believes the half-finished stories of the previous births. One forgets the certainty of future death and destruction. It sees all around people suffer rich and poor alike. But it ignores the potential pain in store for it in arrogance of youth and money. In warmth of youth, it hardly senses the eagle of time flying just above its head.

Slowly world unfolds its true colour. Weather rapidly changes for the worse. Slowly spells of misery stay longer and longer. Drought lengthens. Monsoon becomes a dream. It cuts a sorry figure. Slowly winter of life gets colder and colder. Slowly bodily vigour wanes. Youth wanes. Bones go dry. Colour fades. Sight fades. Shoulder droops. Friends depart. Relations play hide and seek. Earning power comes down. Value in society lowers. Body and mind mock at it. Things fall apart. All holds loosen.

Slowly the cloud of despair thickens. And it realizes the uncertainty of life and the transience of happiness. Slowly happiness becomes rare. Misery abounds. It tries its best to mend the wrinkles and cover the pain from others. It tries this trick, that trick, this medicine, that medicine. But nothing works. Nothing can return the youth. Money and power fail to compensate the depth of despair. Youth looks a distant mirage. Nothing enthuses. World remains same, but its perception towards it undergoes a sea change.

Night of earthly existence darkens the sky of hope. Worries and anxieties deepen. The destination suddenly looks unknown. Doubt develops. Confidence goes lower and lower. To salvage the lost glory, it takes many futile attempts and finally sinks to the pit of despair. The dean and bustle depart. Loneliness becomes the new friend. It can't cope with the fast-changing scenarios of this hitherto unknown phase of life. The path looks desolate. The howling's of death and destructions frighten the solitary traveller. All warmth of bygone youth torments. Life looks grim.

It realizes how unprepared it is to face the new challenges of life. The tall talks on socialism, philosophy, politics, literature take corner seat. It knocks the doors of temples and tries to fathom the mystery of life. But the time is fast finishing out and path looks so long and frightening.

The travel looks uncertain, and the night deepens. All attempts to rejuvenate life fails. Old memories hunts. All things look pale. And it becomes an uphill task to bring life back to track. Now it is forced to face the truth of life.

The real journey begins in hopelessness and pure loneliness. The tryst with destiny nears. Buddha's words so neglected rebound. Spirituality so often relegated to background comes centre stage and a new phase of life begins. One is straightened. The pathless travel begins.

Initially, like a man trying to lift a mountain, illusion looks impregnable. Still the mind in tear doesn't leave hope. Search goes on effortlessly, eyes intently waiting for his return. You have never seen that reality or truth of life yet; waiting is ever on.

Surprisingly, when you feel like leaving the search in despair, comes the mystic call. The eternal truth comes calling you. Life is filled with joy unlimited. Whole world looks different. Body dances. Mind soars. Cosmos sets in mind. Physical cosmos is clearly seen as an illusion. Mind turns the sky of skies. consciousness turns the sky of mind. Truth slowly unfolds. All cosmology, science behind the gigantic creation slowly get revealed. Ego is silenced in infinite love. All complete. All noise disappears. Deep silence and solitude prevail. Millions of books can't describe this state of eternal union.

Nothing connects except the Atman. Once samadhi starts, days on earthly journey are numbered. Ego pretends and acts to be alive to the material world to carry out the remaining work. Earlier, it pretended to be alive to the spiritual world. But the lethal blow is given. Without a fight Atman disarms the uncontrollable ego. Senses come with food but, the eater is lost in another world. Same ego limps in samsara. It settles fast to leave the guest house (body). The mystic dies in its own wonderland! It realizes the purpose of creation! The fragrance of reunion keeps it intoxicated. The divine drug finishes its earthly sojourn.

After the first glance, it takes years to come to terms with old ordinary life. Some memory is erased. Awestruck and unable to communicate what was revealed to it, ego prepares for the return journey. It tries to share the indefinable for the benefit of the struggling seekers. It has seen a goldmine of eternal treasures. Who has words to describe? Slowly samadhi ripens to Nirvikalpa at will.

Every morning it (ego) is pulled infinitely;

And all cosmos devoured within.

Every night at sleep, it pulls back and enters tiny body for a little sleep.

The behavioural effect after realization is drastic. When one and the same consciousness principle is working through all beings, when all are mere instruments at the hands of that all-encompassing, all-powerful, all-pervading consciousness divinity, how can one blame any individual for anything whatsoever? The blame game stops. One has universal compassion even though he knows that all things are his shadows. He has no actions to do, yet he does actions for the benefit of whole creation. Every step of him is to guide his creation to truth. He acts as a divine messenger and torch bearer for his creation. Which side he would take when he knows both killer and killed are not apart from him. He tries to set the highest standards which is forgotten by ruthless and inhuman race for woman and gold. He waits a while and departs. Again, salute to my beloved Atman!!

Through this prayer to my beloved Atman, a few intriguing aspects of our mundane existence are touched on, with an emphasis on remediation. What is the use of wisdom if it fails to ignite eternal hope in the most depressed and forlorn souls? There is no sinner, there is no saint, there is no king, there is no beggar! These are all fake upadhis on the immortal Atman. These are blatant lies we have accepted as our fate! Let us fathom our anguish, our dream, our loss, our curse, our fate with an effort to heal our wounds. We are one, eternal and complete. We are immortal travelers.

ॐ असतो मा सद्गमय । तमसो मा ज्योतिर्गमय । मृत्योर्मा अमृतं गमय । ॐ शान्तिः शान्तिः शान्तिः ॥

CHAPTER ONE

INTRODUCTION

Ego the villain, created and deluded by maya hides and fights in darkness; With dawn of wisdom, it merges in truth. The screen (infinite or substratum) absorbs all characters without itself getting affected; On it rises, matures, and perishes civilizations after civilizations; On it creatures appear, evolve, and go extinct; On it rises and sets time, space, and causations.

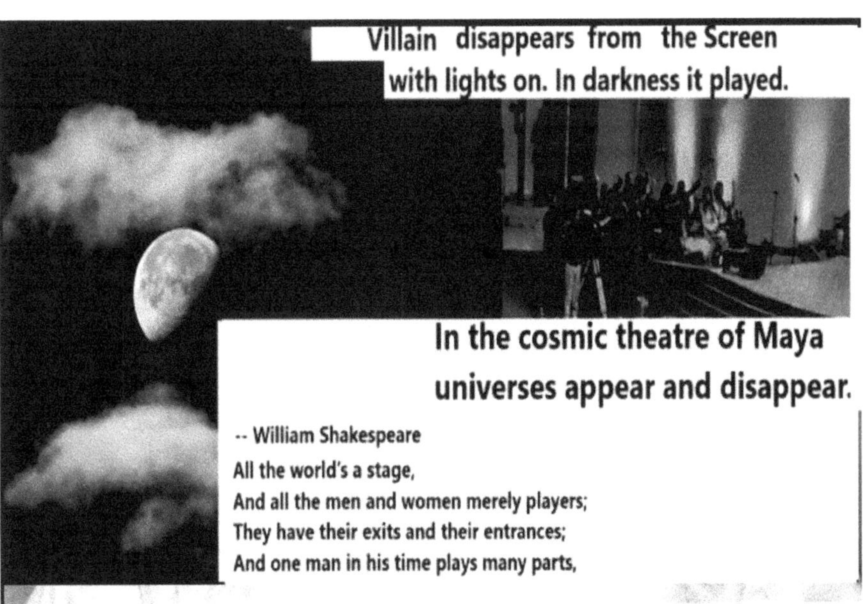

This cosmos is a projection of mind. We all strive to feed our body and mind. But our thirst never ends. We all cycle the wheel of birth and death whether we like or not as long as desire persists.

Vairagya is the key to control the unruly mind. By constant recollection of death, birth, old age, and disease the unruly mind is automatically brought under control. When we focus on the transient nature of our happiness or sorrow, we no more hanker after them. We seek truth.

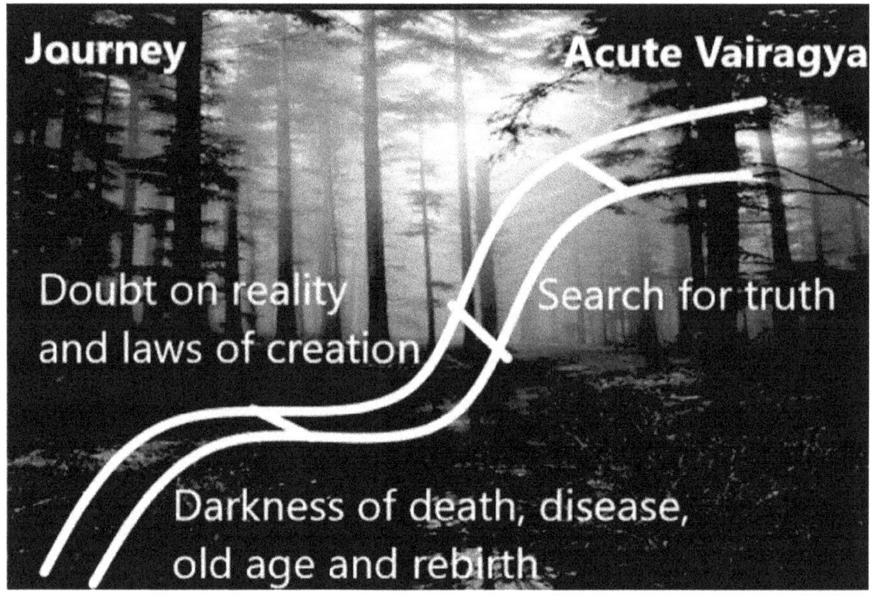

Storm of liberation: Somewhere deep inside the dark cloud of prolonged anguish, appears a little spark of doubt on the reality of this creation; The little spark to thunder and lightening's doesn't take much time for the one who suffers the agonies to the fullest, who swallows each pain as is without a murmur of protest. The undiluted tear is the priceless prayer; It is the highest offering; It touches the most. The little spark if not held supressed shapes into acute vairagya. Indeed, no power can suppress it once it comes to fore.

And it develops into the fiercest storm hitherto unseen and unheard; It is the inner storm of liberation that passes not over a little city but over the whole creation; With what ferocity it grabs the giant bodies difficult to tell; It doesn't leave so quickly till it hasn't devastated the hide outs of illusion. It is a menace; It stays a while uprooting, whirling, and devouring the deepest and age-old roots of avidya; It progresses in silence; It spares nothing; It devours the mass out of all things; It throws away the physical and mental laws; It renders the world into a shadow shed. It is awakening as one wakes up and find whole world is a live dream. Atman alone is, all else false.

Atman or Paramatman or Brahman is one without a second; As soon as ego realizes it is the false Self, it laments. It detaches from body and mind and dies to merge in the Atman. It runs for life it lost in its own noise! Eternal hope returns.

The irrepressible desire for liberation extinguishes all desires for ephemeral things. 'I' expands infinitely and sees whole external nature that eluded for ages is dancing within. Peace and equanimity returns. One becomes complete. One's thirst is extinguished by sublime love. Bliss abounds. All wounds get healed, all creation get intimately connected. All lamenting's, all pangs of separation go for ever. Intoxicated dances the Shiva. Shivoham! Shivoham!

In me rises desire,
In desire rises fire,
In fire rises forms,
Forms entangle awhile,
Forms talk, dance, and disappear.

Ages after in tear,
In me rises the desire for liberation,
That desire burns this desire,
And I expand back as purusha,
Whole prakriti dancing in Me.

Atman alone is:
Ages after, dream starts to end.
The dreamer in delirium; the dreamer at his wit's end;
The dreamer is cornered.
Shipwrecked and forlorn it sank again and again in its own noise;
Who else could be there?
Darkness deepened; Nothing worked; Hope departed; Time flowed;
Helpless it prayed aloud.
Magic happened! All noise gone; Ship rose anew from nowhere.
A subtle voice heard calling; From silence beyond mind came the call.

Who is that called? Could it be captain?

It woke up to find all (creation) gone; It was a dream; It was his dream.

Atman alone is; Atman I am.

In acute pain began the search; In bliss it culminates.

The chapter on Samadhi is a record of different experiences during ascent to Samadhi and descent from Samadhi. When the Samadhi progressing, it is beyond language. The Chapter also focusses on the different kinds of Samadhi especially, the exotic and moksha giving Nirvikalpa one. Whoever enters Samadhi knows what is there in the chapters. All Bhavas are recorded as is to the maximum extent possible. There can't be two different types of realizations. There must be one and only one truth no matter who goes within. So, it affirms what truth is. Truth is profound and enough to silence the noise of the Ahamkara for ever. It laments and prepares for Mahasamadhi. Truth is so powerful that seeker no longer asks for any verification. Can one compare candlelight with the lightening's in cloud? Samadhi is a rainbow of revelations and the seeker dances in the dance of liberation. Ego gets more and more intoxicated as remaining desires die one by one. As the million flood gates of nectar open ego often can't control.

Interestingly, the exit route from samsara is perfectly laid, and the return milestones guide the ego to home. It takes years to come to terms with mundane life after samadhi begins contrary to my original belief. Seeker is still able to finish remaining work although mind, senses and ego are on death bed. Same ego tries to destroy itself not in despair but, in ecstasy. Eternal existence is recalled.

There are rare records of samadhi as it progresses. I hope this brief record instils hope in each seeker desperate for liberation. As samadhi progresses, healing of deep-rooted wounds starts. All wounds heal in Mahasamadhi as body is voluntarily released from the cycle of birth and death for ever.

CHAPTER TWO

BASICS OF SPIRITUALITY

Overview of Realization: The little 'I' expands infinitely as the avarana or cover of maya lifts. One lands in infinite space as infinitely conscious. One escapes from the land of death. One goes beyond thoughts. The infinite pull induces a deep sleep like sublime experience, and all cosmos is seen within the expanded consciousness. Some impurity remains, and over a period gets purged out; And one frequently tastes nectar or Nirvikalpa. The bliss of Brahman overwhelms and all desires to stay in mortal world slowly vanishes. One tries to attain Mahasamadhi or Mahaparinirvana from which, there is no return; One is ever established as truth; One is back as eternally existent; False ego vanishes; Truth prevails; All nectar, all ecstasy, all joys unlimited; All complete, all absolute, all one indivisible eternal whole; There never was a part; The part was a mere illusion, the separation was due to the covering of maya. Once the separation or veil is lifts, there is no two. All Sat-Chid-Ananda.

Withdrawal from the world of mind and senses and slipping away to "silence beyond mind" happens at a very advanced stage. Here, stream of consciousness splits; I-stream races to infinite, leaving mind-stream dipped in carrot (object consciousness). This is pinnacle of meditation.

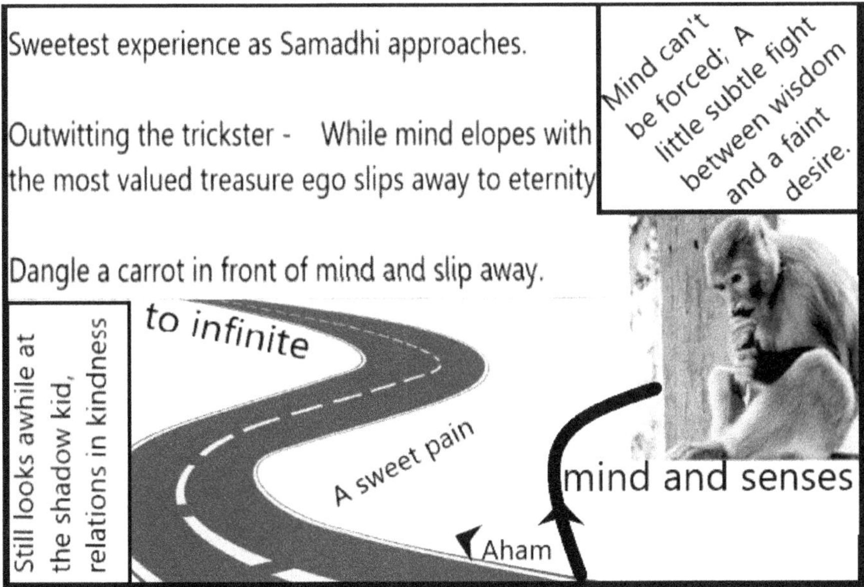

Key aspects of realization are "Time, space, things and events rise and set in mind". "All in Me" is realized. With attention rises the things big or small from memory. With inattention sets the things again in memory. On realization, ego crosses the land of death. As soon as Maya lifts, I-consciousness expands infinitely and can't any longer think of things. Thought drops. Astral travel or experiencing floating in infinite space is realized. One realizes all things as appearances floating within.

One oscillates between the infinitely conscious and finitely conscious for a while. Slowly the Samadhi goes effortless. Nirvikalpa comes when even minute thoughts drop. Million books can't describe this inebriated state of seeker. The bell of liberation rings. The beggar ego prepares to disappear. A very sweet state comes. Wonderstruck, lamenting, and ashamed, remaining slender thread of I-consciousness ascends the mighty ladder of realization. Now, whole earth is nothing before the I-consciousness. Atman disarms the stubborn and invincible I-consciousness in just a glance without a fight. Beloved Atman is all over. How long can one stay with dolls (relations) and sand houses? The dawn of realization is in the sky of liberation. All heavens are crossed. Atman alone is self-effulgent and complete. The grim battle in samsara looks a distant dream. Below picture is an overview of realization as ego is detaching from the land of death and constant worries.

Every finite sight, sound, smell, touch, and smell is after all a thought. Emotions sweet or sour build up around these thought bubbles. And in that non-stop stream of emotions ego gets carried away helplessly. Forced by miseries as ego reflects, one day it holds back and seeks truth.

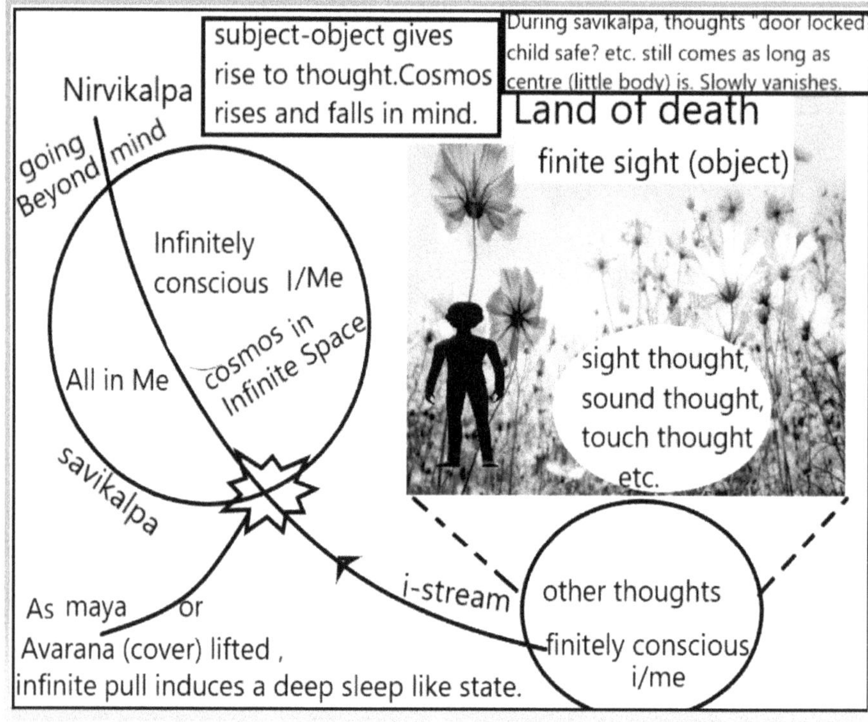

Avidya hides illusive or mithya nature of things. Ignorance of truthis above ego. Ego forgets "I am infinite" burdened by thoughts. As detachment increases, ego recalls "I am infinite ". Seeing back all objects in subject and starting to live on bliss, eliminates the urge for continuing 'I' for the sake of feeding body and mind. As maya lifts, all cosmoses are seen within. Ego sees things rising in attention and falling with inattention. This attention is the presence or I-consciousness that lends life to all images. Seeker sees the transience of all things and recognizes Atman as the eternal companion.

Advaita: Atman or Brahman is not alone or alone-ness. Brahman is subject less, object less, perception less pure infinite consciousness and allegorically referred to as Amrit. 'I' consciously detaches from physical body entering mental and expands to "I am the whole cosmos still aware" before entering Nirvikalpa. As the gate of Nirvikalpa opens, no I, no me, no she/maya, no cosmos, no aloneness, all go indescribable as Brahman or Atman or Advaita or Nirvana or Ananda Vihara or whatever we term it. And, only during descent, the infinitely conscious remember "Oh! I was dissolved in a blast of nectar". Then, the I (super conscious one) contracts and enters (reattaches to) the physical little body as Me. This reattaching is same as rebirth; thus, death process too is indirectly realized. And, most importantly by divine design, this universal memory of the Atman lingers a whole creation.

Value of experience: As many schools emerge and merge, as history gets clouded with misinterpretations (deliberate or not), as one school copies idea from another school, as one school disappears under endless debates, as some believe in inference while others believe in sabda pramana, as internet proliferates, as stories are borrowed, redefined, and resold, it's experience alone that counts. Time is endless; And so is space and his magic.

Four-fold miseries have generated many masters. Books, satsang and scriptures can only supplement, but one who needs truth just as a dying man needs life, would get it. Search like a snake and ladder game takes many births; During acute pain of death and rebirth many superficial learnings disappear and requires re-effort to assimilate the bitter lessons of life. Unless one steps up efforts and desperately runs for truth, the wheel of death continues. Mantras may be used as some pointers to truth. But we must go to the full depth of what is pointed to, and not spoil our invaluable human birth to accumulate pointers. What is the use of knowledge if hunger is not mitigated, and death still hunts.

Love is neither body deep nor mind deep; It is transcendental madness. It is not a flash here and there; it is overwhelming overpowering and eternal. As we navigate through the different lokas or worlds towards truth, we first start with body; One day, fed-up with body we love emotions; There too we fail to quench our thirst; Our hunt continues till we are not swept by the infinite current of truth.

Mukti is dissolution of 'I' ; On one side, the little centre or body to which ego returns, stands like a faint shadow devoured by flood of consciousness; On the other side, the pull of the Atman has taken the little consciousness afar from where return is impossible; Periphery leaves centre; Atman absorbs ego for ever.

Mind, maya, and jagat

As maya lifts, one realizes "on mind and sense consciousness forms the things from mental impressions but appear to come from outside". Law of reflection, light, source of light, and things all spring up in mind from memory. As false seer or ego by force of desire recalls the mental impressions, shapes rise as thoughts. Shapes when attended by physical sense organs appear to be physical. Since we leave bed in morning, organs stay projected throughout day along our attention as objects of sense consciousness. Indeed, we are in a grand magic show. In that magic show, orchestrated in cosmic theatre of maya, rises and flows space, time, and causation. As meditation deepens, jiva lands in infinite space and sees the filling of illusive mass in illusive shapes. This wonder show is the climax of our worldly existence as root of desire gets uprooted. Things are seen as they are!

Surprisingly, 2022 Nobel prize in physics in quantum physics echoes the long-held view of Vedanta. In attention or observation rises things; In inattention they set. They are indescribable when not observed. Adi Shankara referred to this as **"Brahman satya jagat mithya!"**.

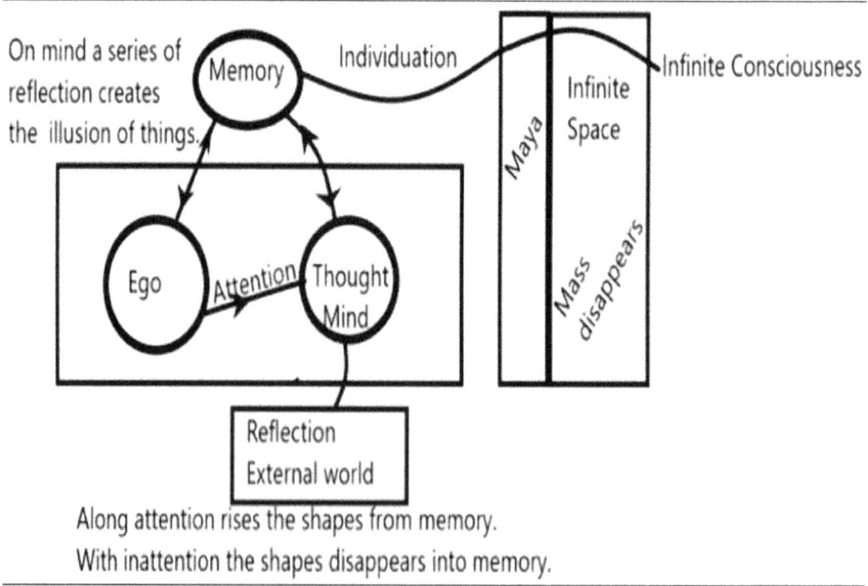

Along attention rises the shapes from memory.
With inattention the shapes disappears into memory.

Why samadhi wipes out all kinds of mortal fears for ever?

Only samadhi insulates Jiva from death and other fears. The very land of death and chaos turns the inner land of ecstasy and love. Can you imagine **walking inside you?** "Yes, it is the wonder of wonders and happens in full awareness. There you see all things as they truly are floating in you; Galaxies are charged with your touch; There you see your tiny shadow like body breathing and walking like a cosmonaut in deep space; You see vegetations, roads, highways, cities all rise, flow, and sink as perceptions; All physical highways over which we ride are seen connecting to infinite; The bends disappear into infinite; One rides as usual while afloat; Your tiny home and bed float in you; There is no gravitation; You are beyond all material laws; Sun touches you; The inner sky of consciousness is seen to be filled with unimaginable faint volumes and shapes divorced of masses".

Can fear touch you?

You move with your action organs through the tunnel of senses just as glow worms move in the depth of night. The trails of glow worms are like the roads you travel externally. The cosmos is silenced in you. You have outgrown all stars and gravitation centres. No black holes can pull you; No sun has power to burn you; And you travel within you; They call it Lokas; You are past all of them; You are past all heavens and hells.

Same helpless Jiva consciously enters the nectarine samadhi field, after losing all physical, mental, object, and subject consciousness as million flood gates of nectar wash it away. Once Jiva descends from samadhi field, there is no more discussion, no more need for approvals, no more doubts, no more fear of death. It has seen the indescribable Atman. All ego's acting's end in one glance and it waits for prarabdha karma to finish. The same ego fixes its own match against its senses and mind as it desperately seeks its svabhav. It holds back from mind and senses!

In the very birth one is fully convinced of rebirth, samadhi is bound to happen. Thereafter, samadhi ripens through a few births in celestial realms called svarga; Mind on death bed, ego in deep repentance, senses can't understand why ego is not receiving alms anymore; Sandwiched between two worlds, the state is indescribable; With no friend, no relation, no interest in planning, it is as if eagerly waiting in a dormitory for the final connecting train to eternity to horn; It sees other passengers are crowded with relatives with bursts of emotions sweet and sour but, it has nobody except the lord of lords the Atman; All Atman here, there, everywhere, and shadows multitudes; World is now a sharp contrast to the poor world earlier.

Three divine messengers are sent to all to win over ignorance. No being ever asks for these three states namely awake, dream and deep sleep, but they are given. Why? Deep sleep state says, "Where goes your worries and things in deep sleep?". Dream state says, "How long you pine for deaths in dream and how long you recall the beautiful things in dream once your dream breaks?" Awake state says, "Why don't you learn from dream and deep sleep states and stop lamenting for external things?". Viveka is the best guide throughout; It is the messenger from truth; Viveka sees what mind, body and ego can't.

See the divine design, reflect deeply on it; Reflect why these triple states are given to all beings unasked; They are there with lower insects to gods to guide seeker back to eternal life; All major schools of spirituality give lots of emphasis on them as divine milestones.

When happens on daily wake up from an absolute point of view?

Daily, when we wake up from sleep, we recall back 'bed, pillow, body, roof, floor, door, window, surrounding, sun etc.' from memory unaware! Contents might have changed since 'last bedtime' as the illusory creation is evolving through other minds as well. You rematerialize, resync and restart engaging your action organs in the ongoing play.

Little address changes to infinite (all address). With lifting of Maya, 'I am this little body-mind' changes to 'I am that whole infinite consciousness in which the whole cosmos appears'. Finally, on complete purification of all subconscious ripples, samadhi ripens to the last uninterruptible stage. No me, no he, no she, no world, only truth as truth. Only Atman is as is. During initial pratyahara practice, fill the necessary thought and keep away from the unnecessary, as it is difficult to practice total withdrawal from both necessary and unnecessary thoughts or things in one go. Whether it is Buddhism or Hinduism experience is the same, only language is different. Example: Buddhist meditation ranges from 1st to 4th rupa dhyana followed by 1st to 4th arupa dhyana followed by animitta chitta samadhi. Brahmin teachers had taught Gautam all the 8 dhyanas and Buddha became Buddha on practicing them to enter the animitta chitta samadhi or permanent cessation of suffering not just elimination of suffering during meditation. Many have got samadhi, many are within, and many will get. Vedas have all the wisdom to be free. It is consistency and desperate desire for liberation is all that matters.

Titiksha

As onetolerates the pain of old age, disease, death, and rebirth, one is closer to truth. In other words, silently suffering the sufferings with reflection leads to Vairagya. Dilution of pain by anaesthesia dilutes bliss as well closing the divine gate of liberation. Effort should be to avoid quick remedies unless necessary.

Transition view of universe from eye of wisdom is strange. Old cosmos where little ego-built nest after nest gets flooded; Cosmos turns a dream enacted within.

Neither rain nor tide, yet all flooded, yet all washed away.

Signs of third eye: One goes speechless! All questions stop! One no more asks because whole world comes inside and there is nobody outside to answer. All questions are answered from within. A beautiful feeling overtakes you. This feeling was never experienced before! Another sky of freedom opens; Not this illusive ever changing physical sky. You see the unseen, be it night, be it day, whenever you recall. These very physical spaces turn dream. Ego is kept absorbed by eternal ecstasy.

You see infinite in broad daylight as the thick cosmic fog surrounds you; You are thrilled not suffocated! The beauty of the design and the designer slowly unfolds, and surrender is the only option before the divine captivator. You die to surrender. You die to catch the attention of that. Such is the grandeur of that. It is impossible to describe unless one has entered that territory. Yes, if the whole world is offered, he would throw away. That is Mukti from the age-old entanglement and fear. Hunger stops. Death no longer comes near. Gratitude, tear, and surrender remains. Only that much ego as required to keep body remains. All karma slowly dwindles!

He is no more attached to any identities no matter how big or small. For him all are brothers and sisters. Love and compassion become his religion! All come under his responsibility. He sides with truth. All ownership and comparison stop for ever.

As the cosmic water slowly floods the valleys of his world, filling spaces after spaces, the same stubborn solid landscapes (our physical earth), where he roamed for ages in fear and hunger, turn into dreamscapes. Same world turns into a beautiful dream.

Ego sees this very world slipping slowly away into oblivion, as the embrace of the eternal gets tighter; Same sun, moon, sky, nature evoke a sublime and strange response from within; All in harmony; All bathed in rapture; Unthinkable experience keeps coming; He tastes timelessness for the first time; He is fully drunk; He feels complete after ages.

Yoga:

By recourse to a simple lifestyle coupled with light asanas, pranayama, and prayer our lost sensitivity to beauty and charm of nature can be gradually enhanced; At the same time automatic withdrawal from many pain points like greed, anger, jealousy, hatred, undue competition, suspicion, impatience, cheating, lying, procrastination, cruelty, ego, bodily lethargy, improper sleep, improper food, indulgence in luxury etc. can be achieved by regular practice. If it is difficult to grasp the below negative example can be used to understand it.

Why   intoxicant or drug is so pleasing for some time?

Because, ego, mind, and senses all remain gathered, focussed, and dipped in a   thread of intense interest, rather than getting   scattered over many mental or physical pain points. There is a forced withdrawal from pain points.

In contrast, during meditation, this withdrawal is not triggered by any external intoxicant.

Taking recourse to intoxicant is a temporary, unnatural, and unhealthy solution while samadhi or realization is nectarine, truly healing and moksha giving. Intoxicant poisons body while yoga heals it.

Journey - Discriminating ego re identifies 'I' with 'eternal witness' not with 'ephemeral body' and then merges with the Atman. And merging must happen consciously before death. Otherwise, rebirth happens. Try to see your own 'dance' from the 'seat of the witness'!

The little sublime snake (discriminating ego) on the neck of lord Shiva is the mellowed down state of the violent ego (the big, hissing, and poisonous one). The witness through Viveka ensures it is mellowed down by the furious forces of nature. In fear it surrenders and then only the game ends!

Enquiry or vichara of "Who am I? Who created this world? Is this world real? Why do I visit this world of sorrows and sufferings again and again?

etc." will remove avidya (ignorance).

Compassion: In ignorance ego identifies, attaches, and claims to own the physical body. Ego is limited. When it sees the infinite existence, it goes mad for dipping in that bottom less ocean of nectar. There lies end to all our endless seeking. That is eternal spring, that is nectar, that is whole, that is aim of all mortals. All boundaries and distinctions automatically disappear. For the really enlightened one, there is no race, no creed, no nation, no boundary, no religion. For the infinitely compassionate one, even animals are as close as the humans. Whole cosmos, animate or inanimate is one indivisible whole.

Viewpoints affect the views. Before maya lifts differences are seen; After maya lifts all are Brahman. Aparokshanubhuti changes everything into ecstasy and perennial love. Mind (effect of maya) which is maya at play is absorbed. In intense vairagya maya lifts. As maya lifts, all things look strange (Brahman satya jagat mithya). Maya is indescribable. "How maya lifts" too is indescribable. As maya lifts, one is thrown into infinite consciousness, and it is impossible to see matter the same old way it was seen before! It takes years to cope with the strange look of the cosmos! Before lifting of maya, mind is hardly seen; After lifting matter is gone. One still can engage with matter but, view is different. It is part engaging with separate parts vs. whole engaging with its integral parts, No jealousy, no fear of loss, no time, no space, no events, no separation.

People in nowadays are so much stressed and conditioned that, the beautiful divine gift "dream state" to indirectly glimpse the heavenly states of existence is missed. Free imagination is not possible even in dream due to sustained burden of awake state. Deep sleep too is not deep enough to taste a kind of samadhi.

Samadhi

As the unforgettable moments of liberation draws closer,
Time to depart from Samsara comes,
Cloud of cosmic awareness thickens to nectar,
False awareness gets thinner,
Mortal enters a dream like state,
All pretensions slowly drop,
Pure message of eternity slowly pours in,
False sensations disappear,
Wonder descends and thrill flows down the spine,
Mystery of his journey slowly unfolds,

The drama rewinds in slow motion,
As the mortal crosses the wonder steps out of causal ocean,
As the lovelorn mortal becomes the love filled immortal.

Samadhi

No nectar no poison,
No pleasure no sorrow,
No heaven no hell,
That (Shiva) alone is supreme,
Recognize That,
Your journey is up to that Supreme,
This journey is to behold eternity,
This journey is the pleasure to see the eternity,
Like the pleasure when home gets nearer after long gap,
In this journey I am every moment with you,
Don't search me only recognize,
I am you; you are me,
I am the end to all the beginnings,
Every end is only my beginning.

Samadhi

When space dissolves in mind,
You are in dream,
When mind dissolves in cause,
You are in deep sleep,
When cause dissolves in Turiya,
Thou become the whole.

Meditation: It is maintaining independence from everything by constantly flowing in one thought "I am verily Brahman"

CHAPTER THREE

REALITY OF CREATION

Is the world real?

The whole cosmos is a projection of mind from memory. The following picture reveals where lies physical matter. Each moment we are navigating in mind from place to place. From memory they rise, in memory they set.

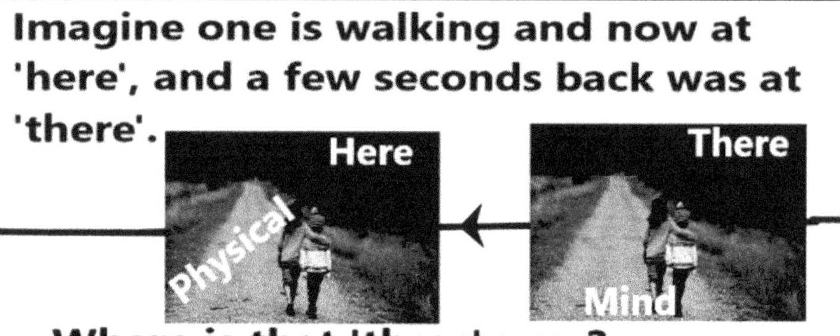

The sound, touch, form, taste, smell all rise as sense consciousness triggering feelings and thoughts in mind and there is nothing that exists apart from hearing, touching, seeing, tasting, and smelling. **What we physically see around lie in mind too.** 'Here' is where physical sense organs are currently engaged. What we call 'There' which is no longer physically visible is really in memory. We move around 'here' and 'there' never aware where 'here' and 'there' really are. They rise and set in mind just as the dream world rises and falls in mind. It is bit difficult to digest but this is truth.

You will be astonished to know the subject matter for which 2022 Nobel prize in physics was awarded. It was awarded in quantum physics and closely echoes the view of Advaita philosophy. The cream of science is echoing the long-held view of Vedanta. We really don't know the true nature of things.

What Adi Shankara loudly proclaimed centuries ago is reiterated through modern physics. Particle behaves in two ways. Particle is both matter and wave. And particle entanglement irrespective of distances is shocking revelations of nature of things. Things are not as they look. Particles separated by trillions of miles instantly influence each other once entangled. This has close relationships to telepathy and other psychic phenomenon that baffles our mid.

What do we mean by thing?

The very things we take as physical look illusive and indescribable on realization. All fights for them are realized to be useless when viewed from a higher level! It doesn't mean our responsibility stops. We are bound by karma and as long as mortal body is there, it needs to be fed and taken care of. But, the fear for loss of things vanishes. World becomes a playground not a battlefield.

In attention rises the shapes and in inattention things disappear. Example: A kid while physically walking with his mother, imagines the frightening image of his teacher in school. 'The teacher in school' is a thought. Thought is a replay of stored impression through the instrument of mind. Even the physical surrounding is a thought.

The post realization days are the sweetest. The noise of ego is not there. Acceptance of situations is quick. One quickly recalls Atman in very tough situations. Rapture rises as intimacy with Atman develops. Ego remains absorbed and intoxicated. There is no loneliness felt. Before realization, we may be in crowd, but at times feel very lonely when we can't connect to anybody. But, during samadhi days no one is there, yet one is at ease with the most intimate inner companion.

All go out (in morning) and return (in evening) to nest(body),
    All lost in emotions plan for future,
    The lone bird (panting ego) neither goes nor returns,
    It is everywhere, it is nowhere.
    There is no mind left to hide,
    There is no Samsara left to play,
    How long to play among shadows?
    The little shadow (own body) grows thinner day by day,
    And bird no more chases shadow; It is free!

Does Brahman really exist? Yes. Brahman alone exists.

How the transition happens? Among several connects and disconnects as the spells come and go, the friendless and detached seeks eternal union. Ego's friends are no friends; Ego's house is no house; Ego's world is no world; Today are tomorrow not. Asangoham! Asangoham!

If Brahman exist, then in what form and where?

Yes, as the all-pervading pure infinite consciousness.

Does God exist? Yes, but within mind. What we take as external is internal. So, it hardly matters whether the object of worship is external or not as goal is the same. Means may be different.

Where does God stay?

God exists in mind. Cosmos floats in mind.

What Afterall is this creation?

A mirage or a dream orchestrated through power of Maya.

What is the purpose of this creation?

To play well and go back home (realization).

CHAPTER FOUR

GOD, MAYA, REBIRTH

God does exist call it internal or external. Cosmos is projected by God through the power of Maya. There is nothing wrong in worshipping idol or form or guru as sudden and direct jump to the Nirakara or formless aspect of truth is almost impossible in the beginning of search. Meditation on the formless is for the very advanced seekers.

We mostly need a base or adhara to pull the distracted mind back and then hold the mind gathered around the base. Even the external idol is after all internal only as clearly revealed latter. Atman is beyond heavens and hells. Gods in heavens too meditate seeking escape from the wheel of birth and death. Karma decides where the next birth happens. Some births are favourable for realization while others are not. Keep praying wherever possible.

Another very important aspect of creation is external worlds whether heavens or hells are all illusive and spread in infinite space. Infinite space is the internal state of cosmos. It is invisible, undifferentiated, and not conditioned by mind. Creation happens in infinite space. Infinite space is the causal ocean. Only the illusive seeds or memory remains as one lands here in meditation. Individual mind projects individual things out of it. Universal mind projects cosmos in it. Mental waves slow down here. As mental waves rise matter rises. After Maya lifts, infinite space is visible. Seer of infinite space is infinite consciousness. Whole cosmos is clearly seen as a massless illusion with illusive lines of separation in infinite space. This **illusive view or seed** suddenly gets condensed and contracted back to so called external things once seeker gets distracted again. This is the key fact. Limited mind fails to see the whole, and separated it cries and fights. Ego is silenced when pulled away to infinite space. There remains nothing for it to grab. And it gets peace of deep sleep.

For seekers on earth, universal memory is realized at a very advanced stage, and only then poor Jiva sees the mesmerizing creation in full. Before that one wheels the cycle of birth and death. Absorbed in a few finite sights and taking them to be its little world, ego roams from birth. Like cattle grazing this field that field, senses graze a few things. When recall is deep, one enters the mystical zones of creation. God, heavens, hells all really make sense. Where can death hide? Its hide outs are seen.

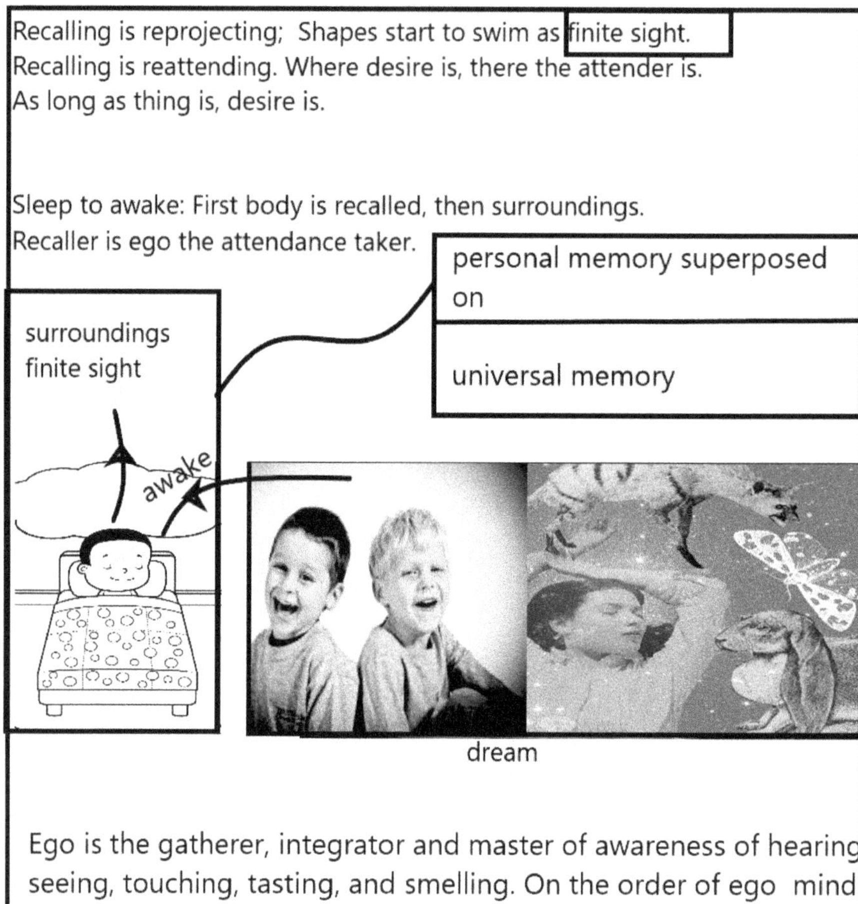

As jiva wakes up from sleep, it recalls its personal memory and projects the surroundings as a series of finite sights and finite sounds. First thing to be recalled is body. This personal memory when corrupted Jiva is diseased. The organs are not in rhythm when personal memory is not coherent. All the repairs and operations by medical experts happen at the level of personal memory. Personal memory is not in brain organ, rather brain organ is projected from personal memory.

As dream worlds are false and valid for a dream, the personal awake time worlds experienced by Jivas are false although the duration is a lifetime. Universal memory is realized at a very advanced state. Telepathy and other neuro symptoms defying medical worlds occur at universal memory level. The siddhis and the siddhas too have some indirect access to universal memory. In samadhi, the whole cosmos is opened just as in a medical lab the body is opened by advanced experts.

Heavens: As seeker evolves, love for life increases. As seeker evolves mental love overrides physical cravings. And one enters higher and higher heavens with bodies which linger for millions of years without ageing. Mind turns subtler, lighter, and calmer. Still death comes, still dukkha remains. Still uncertainties and helplessness remain. Still ego strives for others' approval. Still ego strives for union with its much cherished beloved and keeps dreaming for more and more.

Rebirth: Desire pulls ego back to the wheel of birth and death by detaching from one body and reattaching to another body. In the valleys of own mind, it roams in search of pleasures. Just as we forget awake state once within dream, so too it forgets its past life. Worse still, it doesn't even believe there is after or before life! It hardly knows that mind is an endless magical substance that keeps on stretching with desire accumulating more and more impressions, thus getting fatter and duller birth after birth. And the desire to explore it more and more simply traps ego.

Unfulfilled cravings force I-consciousness to hop from body to body. It recreates its own new body from past impressions and will power. It rebuilds its own body like a carpenter builds a tool. Yet, it asks "How death comes? How rebirth happens? Who created me? Who created others?".

Seeking: Millions of lives after, in sustained pain actual tear flows. It becomes inconsolable. Helpless and broken it moves like a corpse cursing no body but itself. It seeks answer to death, birth, old age and death. It tries to recall its real bhava. It prefers solitude. It laments and withdraws from the madding crowd's ignoble strife. It asks to itself 'Who am I?' Search deepens. World slips away from mind. Things fall apart as its centre is split. Things lose their shining as ego tries to see them, evaluate them, critically assess their originality not flowing with them. And it crosses many milestones, each day bringing new hope, eager to know how many are still left.

Faith returns. Rebirth looks a fact not a possibility. Own pain opens its eyes. It feels others' agonies. It turns compassionate. Universal love returns.

It recognizes nature. Its harmony with nature is restored. And will see truth comes like a storm. Vairagya, Bhakti, Karma, Gyana are all explored as it inches towards truth.

And amid true frustration and true joy the **lightning strikes.** Maya lifts. Mind itself becomes Drysya. All the valleys it roamed life after life is seen back floating within. And it enters the avyakta space of truth. And it recognizes all bodies as images in a movie. It wakes up from its own dream. Wonder after wonder unfolds.

Body is ever part of Prakriti. It is mind alone that draws the line between me and others. It is mind alone that thinks itself to be different from others. Sense organs are mere mouths, enjoyer is mind.

Who am I?

I am the Atman.

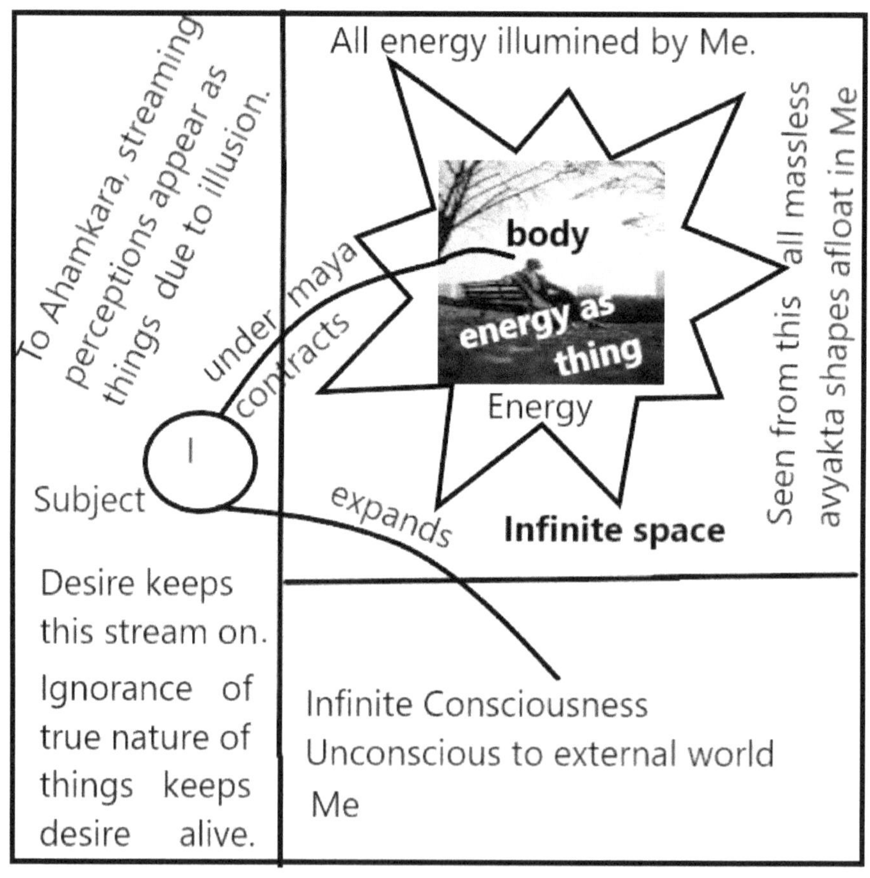

I am pure infinite consciousness ever detached ever free. External world is not apart from Me. Giant far away galaxies are but my expansion. They rise and set in infinite space. I expand to infinite space. In infinite space rises the bubbles of memory. And around the bubbles revolve the beings unaware of who they really are fighting and in tear. Being generally refers to both body and mind. Body is simply a projection of memory by mind. Desire decides the projection in the direction of attention.

The Mandukya Upanishad says "Atman is the silence beyond mind". The Atman or real Self has four aspects through which it operates. They are awake, dream, deep sleep, and Turiya (4th).

Waking or gross: In this state, I-consciousness is turned outward called the external world. Through 7 instruments and its 19 channels as I-consciousness, it experiences the gross objects of the phenomenal world. The instruments are the macrocosmic elements behind creation while the channels are the microcosmic individual being.

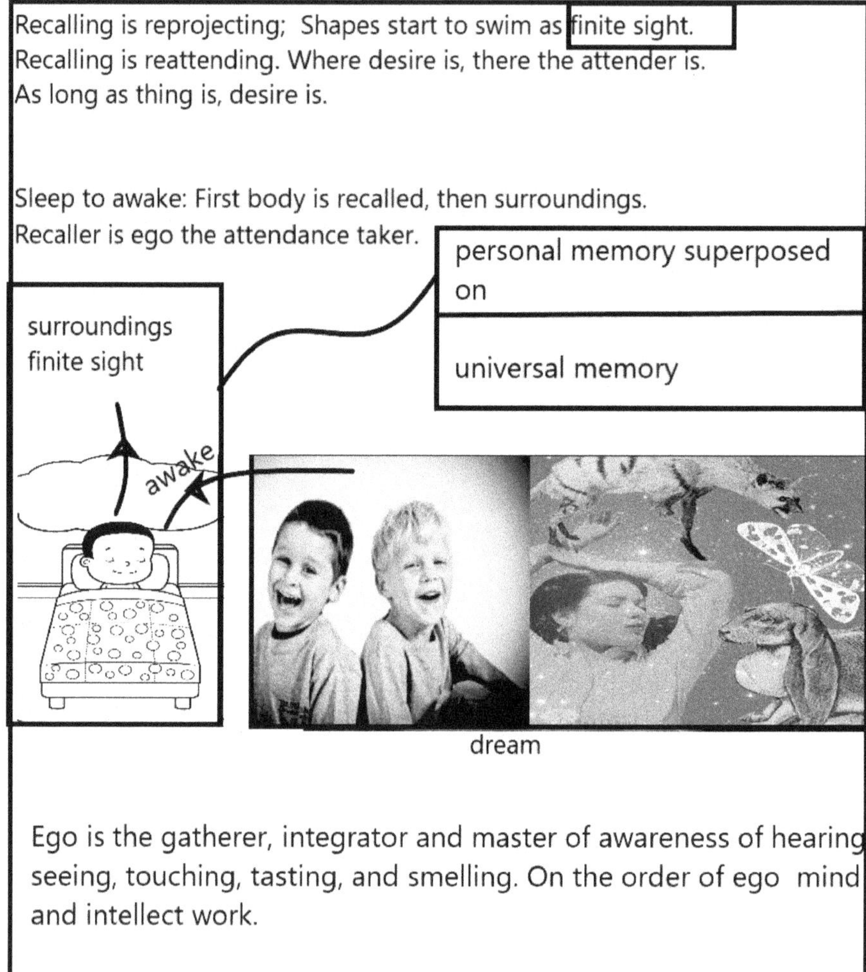

Enter Caption

Seven instruments: First consciousness through the power of maya manifests outward as space, air, fire, water, earth along with the individuation from the whole and the flow of energy (which we know as the pulling impulse towards breath).

Nineteen channels: The individual operates through mind, memory, ego, and intellect. These four operate through 5 vayus, 5 active karmendriyas, and 5 cognitive senses.

The 4th aspect is Turiya in which I-consciousness is neither turned outward (external world) or inward(dream). Rather, the I-consciousness expands infinitely and sees what really it is. It is beyond both cognition and non-cognition. Turiya is silence beyond mind. This is pure and infinite consciousness or the real Self, ever serene, ever tranquil, and ever existent without a second. This Self is to be realized. All three states come and go in this 4th.

Who created the cosmos? Gods in higher mind or heavenly planes of existence. The causal layer is laid with the help of Maya. Ego's as temporary units of separate existence are implanted as seeds. Individual mind projects subtle and gross from the seed.

When and how the creation started?

It is infinite and through expansion of the power of Maya. Maya has no beginning. Below is a description of creation as per Hinduism. Spiritual worlds are the highest. Innumerable material worlds swim in the causal ocean. By Vairagya or Bhakti or detached Karma ego expands beyond the material worlds as Maya lifts. As Maya lifts, ego is beyond the spell cast by Maya, that is it is out of the causal ocean of cause-effects. The divine wisdom attained is referred to as Brahmajyoti. Life is eternal in spiritual worlds. The distance between seer and seen is in material worlds. Spiritual worlds are beyond thoughts. There love is eternal, union is ever on.

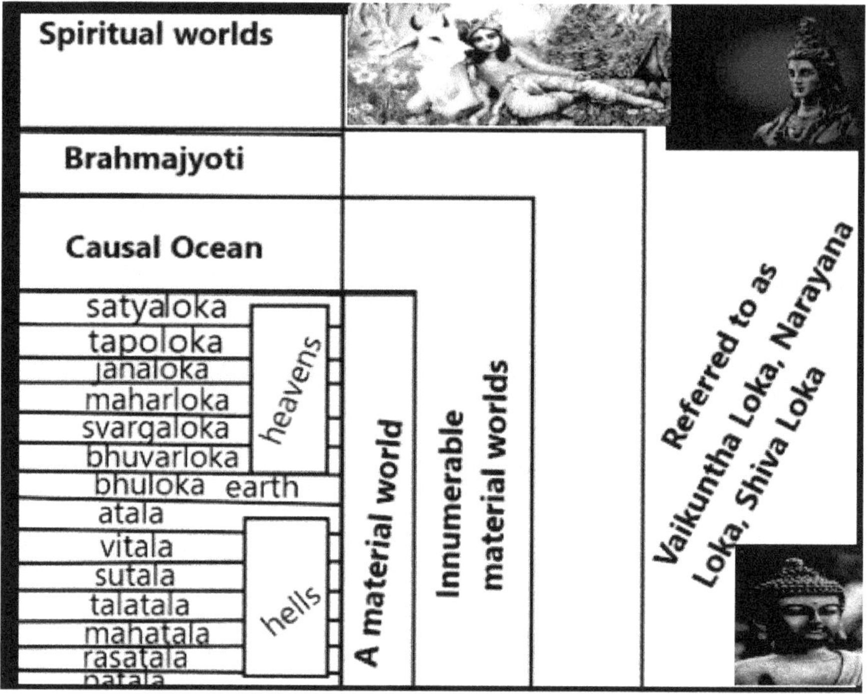

Below is a description of creation and levels of enlightenment as per Buddhism. The creation spread across different Lokas is infinite. In the light of Arupa desire gets controlled. One no more comes under desire. Vairagya directly helps one land in Arupa Loka directly from earth. Arupa Loka is a mighty meditation plane experienced in Samadhi. Sign of entry in Arupa is all cosmoses seen within swimming like fishes swimming in water. Ego's days are numbered.

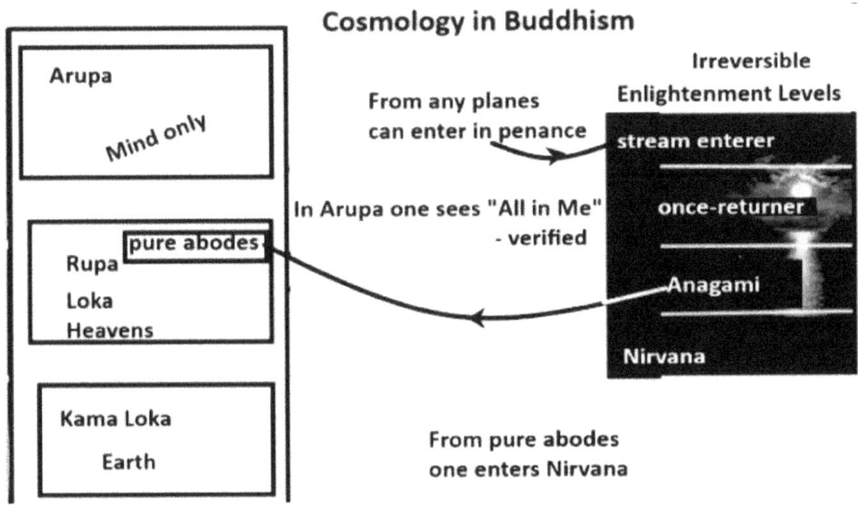

We are in Kama loka or as per Hinduism in Bhur Loka. From human birth, all states of existence are reachable through meditation. An advanced yogi right from earth, can travel to planes 28-31 and realize what it is to be in mind-only state. It too can experience plane 22 where mind is totally suppressed while having a dream-like body. Lower planes of hellish existence are known to all in kali-yuga as social, economic, and religious chaos bring to surface the animalistic planes of existence right in human plane (Muladhara to Sahasrara). In planes 23-27, the subconscious ripples die due to combination of wisdom (attained in 28-31) and instant ability to fulfil any desire with a powerful live dream like power. Hinduism too has a very well laid out explanation of Trilokas as given above.

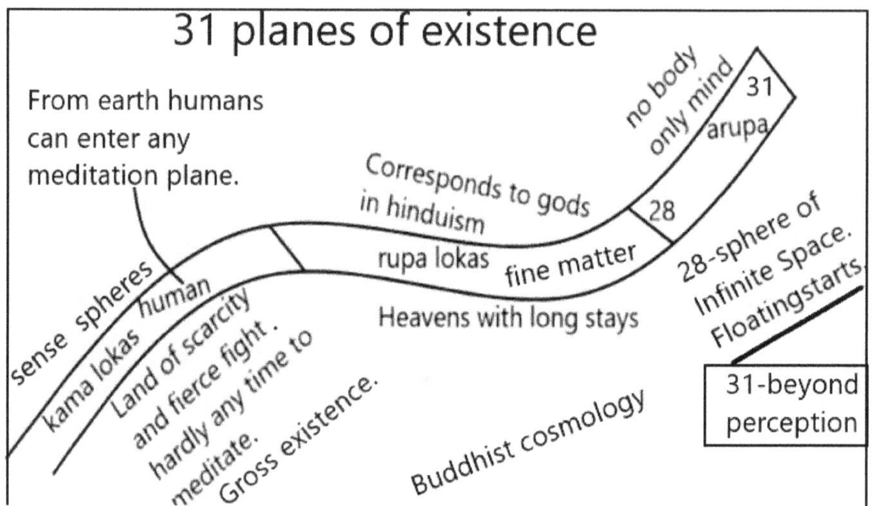

With the onset of Samadhi, the view of existence changes from material to immaterial. View goes more and more sublime and profound. Wonder thickens; Continuous flashes of lightening pierce and tear apart the dark cloud in full; All are ablaze in wisdom; Subconscious raw trunks of tree of desire too burn into ashes.

With entry in mental layer (of Panchakosha), one sees all things rising in mind from memory. Floating starts as identification truly shifts from body to mind. Still deeper, as dharana deepens, one sees shristi implanted as the primordial seed; Further deep, the blast of nectar wipes away the cause (maya's seed or desire) as the fortunate one is re-established back as Brahman.

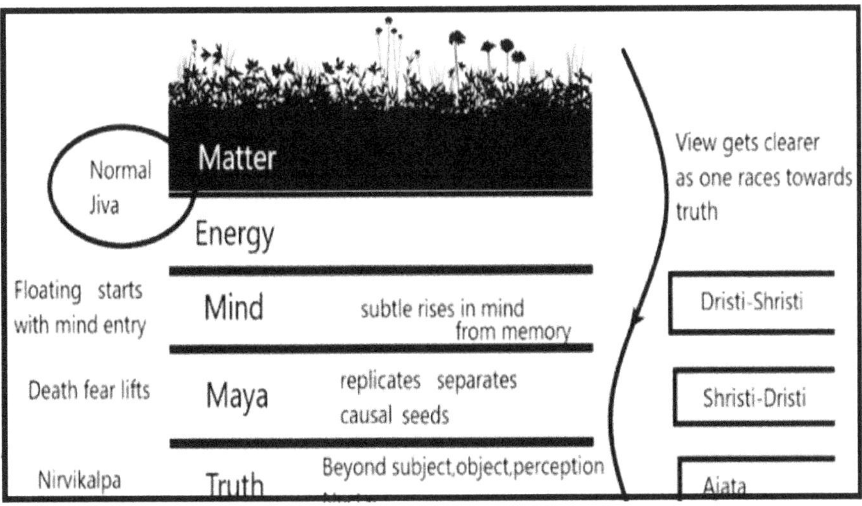

Stung by nectar ego unwinds and resorts to lap of eternal love, freedom, and existence. Not even one remains with you as you ascend the top of the ladder of existence. No need to be surprised. All undesirable elements go. Intoxicated and inebriated ego asks, "Devour me in full."

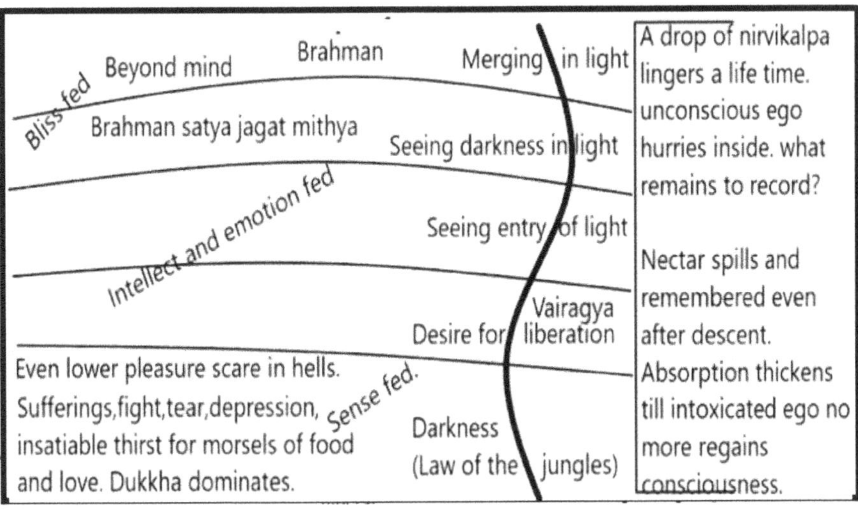

AsangOham asangOham asangOham punah punah
sacchidanandaroopOham ahamevaahamavyayah

Unattached, unattached, unattached am I, again and again; of nature eternal existence-knowledge-bliss am I; I am That. That am I, which is the irreducible, immortal, endless factor.

What is time? A perception.
What is space? A perception.
What is Matter and Energy?
A stimulated mental formation.
Are there heavens and hells? Yes.
What decides our entry into heavens and hells? Karma.
Does world ever get destroyed? Yes.
Who destroys it and how?
Forces of nature automatically do it.
Is Maya behind this creation? Yes.

Maya: She is the first to be born in manifestation and last to recoil back to Brahman after whole manifestation dissolves. Maya is lifted in acute vairagya. Avidya (attachment to things taking them as real) finishes as one sees what things truly are. Mass and material laws vanish as one lands in infinite space. All world is caught as shadows, as a cosmic dream.

I see how my shadows (worlds) get lit up, like a city getting lit up once electricity comes! The order
in which they are lit up is the hierarchy or cosmology or tree of creation. When I tamper the highest through my Gods, the lowers collapse. All laws are illusions, all bodies giant or small are illusions. Like flowers budding and fading in a garden, I see (in Savikalpa) the lokas or worlds or planes of existence rising and falling in me. Even during descent from Nirvikalpa, when I am still well past the highest heavens in infinite space (the inner state of my cosmos), I can't catch Her (my power, my beloved Maya); She evades. I see her works painting illusions (skeleton of creation including Gods which Nasadiya Sukta is referring to) on Me. I am thrilled as the paintings (illusions) are rendered on Me in Savikalpa state. So, She is before

the creation, and She is after the creation is swallowed. She is the wonder behind all wonders! Salute to Her! Probably this is the reason, the great Buddha remained silent on some of the intriguing questions on creation. Even the lifting process of Maya is not seen by the one entering samadhi; Such is the beauty of creation, graver than the gravest, the wonder of wonders! Marvelous! All revealed only on Mahasamadhi!

Nasadiya Sukta (Hymn of creation):
There was neither non-existence nor existence then;
Neither the realm of space, nor the sky which is beyond;
What stirred? Where? In whose protection?
There was neither death nor immortality then;
No distinguishing sign of night nor of day;
That One breathed, windless, by its own impulse;
Other than that there was nothing beyond.
Darkness there was at first, by darkness hidden;
Without distinctive marks, this all was water;
That which, becoming, by the void was covered;
That One by force of heat came into being;
Who really knows? Who will here proclaim it?
Whence was it produced? Whence is this creation?
Gods came afterwards, with the creation of this universe.
Who then knows whence it has arisen?
Whether God's will created it, or whether He was mute;
Perhaps it formed itself, or perhaps it did not;
The Supreme Brahman of the world, all pervasive and all knowing
He indeed knows, if not, no one knows
—Rigveda 10.129

What is perception?
Perception is stimulated mental impressions,
Energy is the stimulant, supplied by desire.
Time and space are perceptions,
Things are streaming perceptions;
Things rise, flow, and disappear with inattention.

Maya is indescribable, yet its effects are the trigunas.

What are the powers of Maya?

Maya divides the Infinite into finite shapes and forces. Maya functions through its two powers: the power of projection and power of concealment. Power of projection involves vikshepa, distraction and mental wandering; Maya conceals from us Brahman, the fundamental oneness of everything and everyone in the universe. Maya is that which makes the whole appears as part, the infinite appears as finite, the formless appears as form. Maya seemingly divides the undifferentiated consciousness so that the object is seen as other than the self. Maya fashions the world.

On whose command maya works? Is there anybody apart from the Brahman?Only in Samadhi one gets answer to it. It is beyond words.

Is Karma supreme? Yes. There (liberated state) no other to help; There no others to blame. Yet, karma rules here (samsara); Yet karma opens the gate to there; It is karma that decides our fate.

Is there any rebirth? Yes. The I-consciousness flows from memory as a new mind-body; Unaware it again entangles in familiar grounds to settle old dues. It meets old relations in new bodies but can't recognize. In long pains of death and rebirth, it forgets its old associations. From old memory, I-stream flows again, unaware of what really it is, and where really it is.

What happens after death?

Body mingles in nature. Journey of 'I' continues.

What reincarnates, why and how?

Ego continues its journey if desire exists. As fire of vairagya burns the supply to conscious, subconscious surfaces; Subconscious too burns; The supply is "wealth plan, to be born again, recognition, pleasure, greed, bad feelings for others etc".

CHAPTER FIVE

PHILOSOPHIES

What are the various paths to realization?

If a stream has force, it will meander through all difficult terrains to reach ocean. As long as unquenched thirst is, as long as wound is, search is. Path opens on its own when tear is unending. Search is as old as sufferings and not specific to a learned and privileged few. Who is not searching? Who is not meditating from a deer in the jaws of a lion to a diseased human being gasping for a little breath?

Doesn't he feed his insects with as much love as he feeds the humans? Is there a creature he doesn't feed considering low, dull and sinful? His sun is for all, his air is for all, his light of wisdom is for all. Like a mother, like a father, he loves his entire creation with extreme compassion. Million gurus garbed as nature, as serving and kind humans, as situations, as pains guide his creation to truth. Who knows in what different ways he guides all to truth? Only he has power to take care of his limitless creation. What we invent, what we prophesise, what path we discover, what religion we create are nothing new to him.

How can the grand creator forget the purpose of his creation? He has given us dream, deep sleep and awake states coupled with conscience and intellect so that we can reflect on them in pain to find truth. Did we ever ask for these three natural states? We create a rocket and try to forget him in pride. Death doesn't spare anybody. All are same in his creation. Our show of ego is our enemy. We must be human to see the tear of others; We must be kind to take care of his dumb creatures; We must love and serve his creation for the sake of love if we want his grace.

However, some familiar paths followed by seekers all around are Karma Yoga, Bhakti Yoga, Ashtanga Yoga, Middle Path, Jnana Yoga, Kriya Yoga etc. All lead to same result. Acute vairagya is not contrary to Bhakti; The last gate opens in bhakti or love; Unconscious to this world Jiva enters Nirvikalpa.

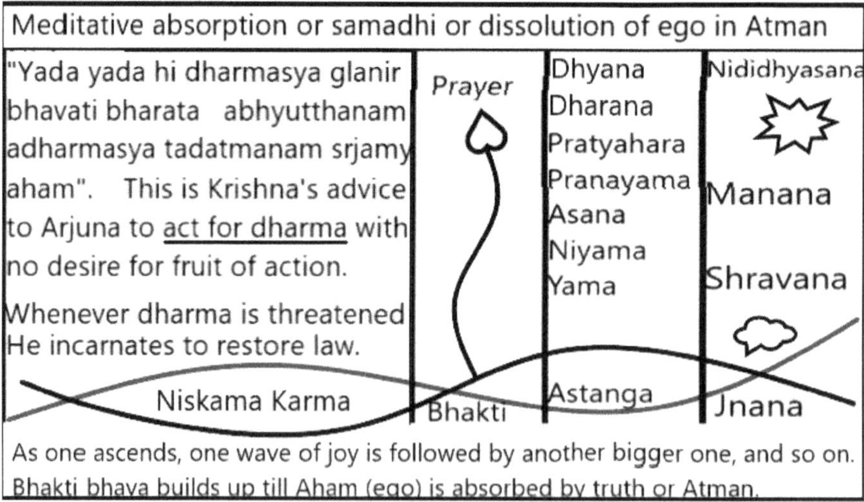

Wonder is magician (ego) can't see magic anywhere in the land of magic! More wonder is it runs after other magicians to do magic for it for attaining magical wealth! "Cries the almighty in the jail of flesh and blood;

Limited, blinded and wounded, all its magical powers forgotten chasing hunger. Can magic food ever satiate its magic hunger?". So, the wheel of death rolls on as long as it takes magic as real. Why hunger returns after eating? The doubt on the design of material creation must develop triggering search for truth. "Something is wrong somewhere and I am helpless to find it out." opens the gate to freedom. Recognizing the problem to be solved is important. Complacency due to mere theoretical understanding is not the answer. The pain in womb due to long wait for parts to be composed is enough to erase mere surface understanding. Deep effort for a real solution gets carried through lives.

If this world is full of sorrows and sufferings then, why is this creation?
Heavenly planes of existence are joyful, although death is still there. But, from lower spheres of existence life is filled with continuous sorrows and sufferings. This creation is a magic; Due to unawareness and forgetfulness being is so much entangled that the flawless and majestic creation appears burdensome. With realization, one knows "Why this cruel creation?".

Is there a way out of this vicious circle of birth and death? Yes.

What is the famous theory of dependent origination? This is the cause-effect model of our existence and for every effect there is a cause. And, on uprooting of ignorance, the 11 subsequent links that chain the creature in the vicious circle of birth and death get broken one by one. One realizes truth and attains Nirvana.

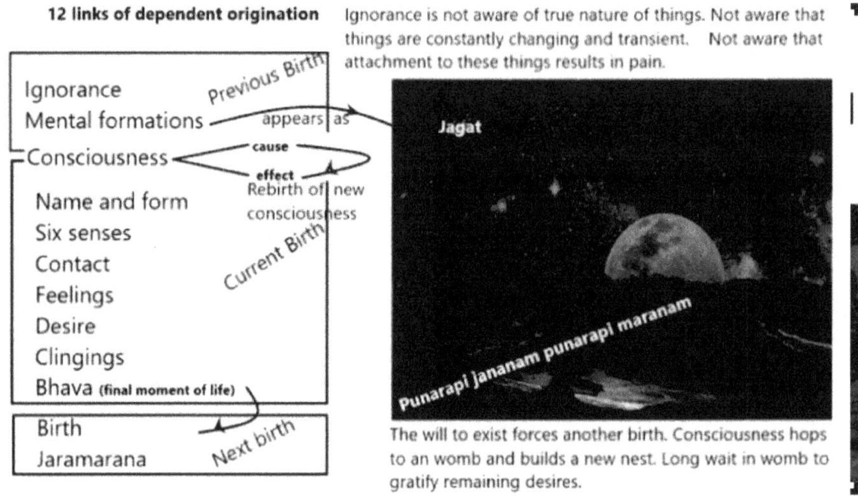

The will to exist forces another birth. Consciousness hops to an womb and builds a new nest. Long wait in womb to gratify remaining desires.

Eternal traveller, and stages of its journey: Lifting of maya starts with entering a transition state as 1/2 maya, and 1/2 Eshwar, allegorically referred to as Ardhanariswara (a form of lord Shiva). From this highly meditative state one can communicate both to the myriad Jivas trapped in time and space as well as to the sphere of Atman. How can otherwise one realize Maya without (re)becoming that at least partially? Whole prakriti is in an infallible embrace with the nectarine purusha. Purusha as infinite 'I', realizes that it is dreaming, and cosmos is a live dream; And He was within the dream as a little Jiva chained by His own Prakriti; Purusha as infinite 'I' realizes that She (the inert principle or illusion referred to as 'seen' aspect) is 'I' alone taking care of the dream kids crying and laughing; He is She and She is He; Samadhi ripens to Mahasamadhi and Jiva wakes up fully awakened, slipping away to eternity unable to resist the flood of bliss; One is non-dual Atman the one Self of all.

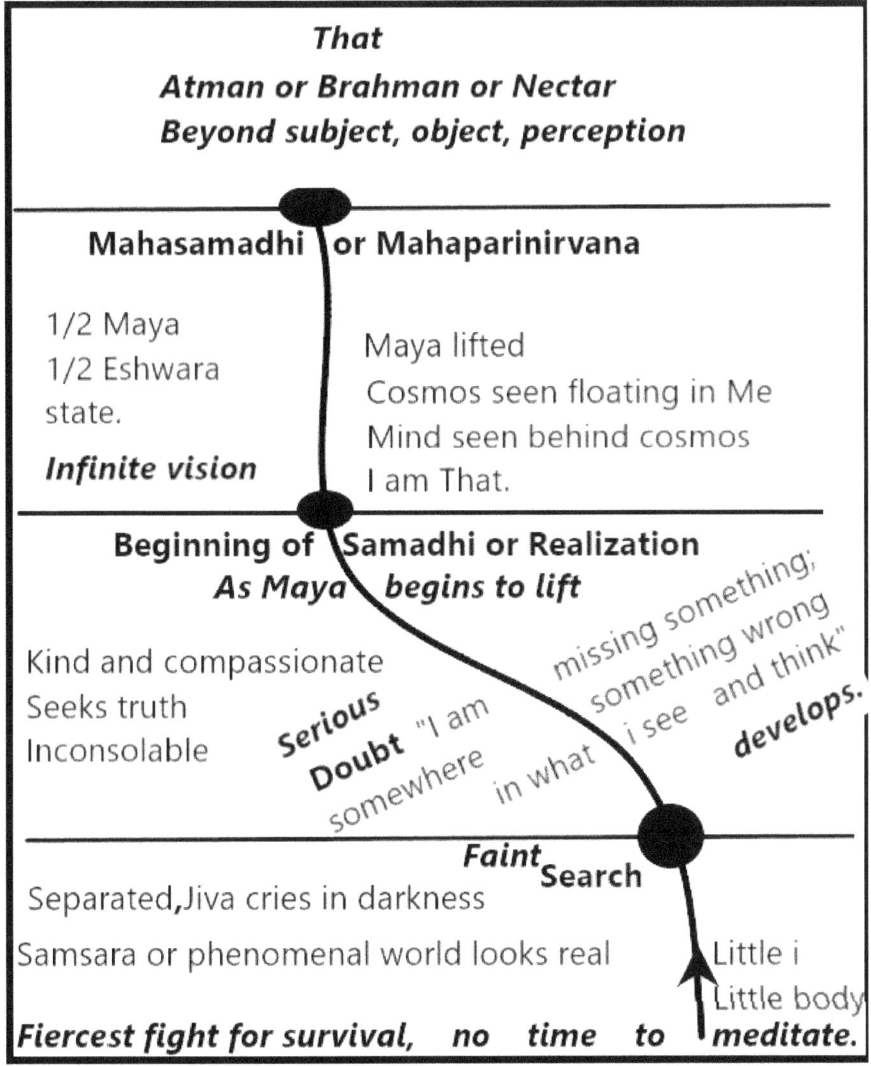

No need to harm others to impress somebody. Who after all is really yours for ever you are so busy to impress? Be neutral, be detached, take sufferings as a way to find him. Be grateful to him. No matter what path we follow, no matter what colour we are born with, no matter what nations we are born in, we are oneness after all. We all are the same oneself of all infinite, ever pure, ever complete and ever blissful. Ignorance of who we really are creates panic. Separation breeds fear. We are lost in the jungle of Maya. A little light is the major need. Just gather a little grain of faith and always bow to that unknown creator. Tear is prayer, suffering is offering, love is grace. Never be cruel, for who the hated one we never know. Who knows may be in some life the very hated one was a close relation so much adored and cared. Love all. Gratitude is love.

Who are some famous saints? Lord Buddha, Mahaveer, Ramakrishna Paramahansa, Adi Shankaracharya, Ramana Maharshi, Mira, Sri Chaitanya etc. have graced our earth in recent times while the list is long. Many have realized and many will realize. In infinite space and time beings come and go. Whoever steadfastly practices while remaining in the righteous path and company can attain. Nothing is impossible for a genuine seeker. The ones acting to be spiritual never reach there in ages.

The famous mantras and mahavakyas from Vedas and Upanishads directly transport one into the land of eternal joy if reflected properly and followed consistently. Consistency and faith are the key. Clouds of despair can be exploited to open the door of eternity instead of being overtaken. Lord Buddha used reflection on suffering as a potent weapon to end the suffering itself.

Meditation is not merely attending a few workshops. They help, but you have to help yourself by continously walking the path irrespective of thousands of obstacles.   As you think, so shall you become.

Some good materials I use to keep my soul absorbed when samsara tries to tear me into pieces by so many distractions.

Nirvana Shatkam, and Bhaja Govindam by Adi Shankara.

Krishna Bhajan

Ram Bhajan

Buddham Saranam Gacchami

Mahavakyas like Tat Tvam Asi, Aham Brahmasmi, Ayam Atma Brahma, Prajnanam Brahma, ekam evadvitiyam brahma, sarvam khalvidam brahma, so 'ham.

अष्टवक्र गीता , Bhagavad Gita, Mandukya Upanishad

Mahabharat
Ramayana

Ramkrishna Paramhans

Ramana Maharshi

The Vairagya Shatakam, or the verses on renunciation, by Bhartrihari.

ॐ पूर्णमदः पूर्णमिदं पूर्णात्पूर्णमुदच्यते । पूर्णस्य पूर्णमादाय पूर्णमेवावशिष्यते ॥ ॐ शान्तिः शान्तिः शान्तिः ॥

त्वमेव माता च पिता त्वमेव

Meera Bai	Tulsidas Bhajans
Kabir Das	Swami vivekananda
Gurunanak	Yogananda

Nirvana Shatakam of Adi Shankara summaries the answer to the question "Who am I?". Sometimes, continuously troubled by four-fold miseries, mind no longer connects to charms of Samsara. If this pain develops and intensifies, it is called Vairagya. The storm of vairagya regathers the dissipated mental and physical energies and uproots even the subconscious desires for things.

Door closed from within

    Towards the end of sadhana,

    As fire of intense vairagya rages,

As the fire burns the forest of avidya,
As maya lifts for ever,
Nothing remains,
A vast inexpressible shadow flows in internal sky of liberation.
As the shadow merges in akhanada mahalaya,
The final question of causation vanishes,
Nectar remains wrapped in nectar,
Mind folded, door closed from within.

Mind control:
This mind is poison; This mind frees.
This mind is hell; This mind is heaven.
This mind is maya at play, this mind projects this body.
This mind if forced kill's the body!
How can we transcend mind?
Vairagya is the key. It cleans all mental formations.

As desire wanes, mind rejects same objects.
Same flower fades: Same body gets old, writhes in pain and decays.
Same colour fades; Same sun sets; Same moon wanes.
Same house lies dilapidated; Same road forgotten; Same brothers fight.
Same body looks old, same love wanes.
Desire remains; This is samara; All transient, all come and go.

We hardly know the path of the divine. In scolding's, miseries lie hidden the immortal messages. Let the worst pass, let the tempest subside, let the filth called body gets its due, let the ego-mind-senses run riots Life is the soul the immortal unity ,the inseparable whole. Earth a mere transit point, heavens are millions and millions of times longer and soother. Imagine, cosmos if filled only with misery is purposeless and that's not the case. Miseries are battles and winner is Atman.

The intense call for absolute freedom from all kinds of fear connects the seeker to infinite. Half-hearted prayer or show of devotion is useless. Be genuine to yourself. Cry genuinely for truth. Truth reveals. Storm of liberation uproots deep rooted desires. Many regular works halted as the storm passes , raging its fury over the cloud of despair devouring the subconscious. With what speed it crosses which instrument can measure? With what sound it roars who has capacity to measure? It finishes all plans; it lifts giant galaxies like dry leaves. Roaring oceans go inaudible. The creation is silenced. All cosmoses turn shadows. Cry out loud for freedom. One loud call is enough to connect to eternity. You have been here before crying and lamenting. But passion for world has overshadowed passion for truth. And you have returned empty handed back to the land of death.

Side with truth. Nothing helps when kala hunts. Let tear flows. In many lives other animals have eaten our flesh live. We as humans are much better placed as compared to animals roaming in jungle in fear. Why compromise with pain unless inevitable? Titiksha is important. This human birth is rare. Be genuine and innocent. Truth or Atman alone has power to overcome dukkha for ever. We seek in pain and dissolve in bliss. Time and space are two temporary magical planes yoked and unyoked to the Atman through power of Maya. Maya is revealed to you when you exit from her theatre or world.

They silently force one to start on the eternal pilgrimage.

Is truth so costly? Who can't afford a simple and mindful living? Who is deprieved of beholding a full moon running in cloud? Who is stopping us from reflecting on sufferings? If no has conquered death, disease and old age then what is the point in avoiding them? Who tells to listen to fake stories of successful avoidance of old age?

Service to mankind is service to god. It is the easiest path to liberation.
See oh mind! No acting, serve for love's sake!
In land of magic scarcity an illusion; In land of magic desire can't be.
Icy hand of greed stole its (ego) magic wand,
leaving it trembling in hunger.
All his maya, all his test.
Yet, as belly burns, his creation is in pain.
His million hands feed his millions:
Ego's hands only two, too tiny yet too strong.
Serve all with gratitude and humility,
Whose wealth? Today ours tomorrow gone.
Bow down with folded hands,
See them pour out their hearts, see them burst into tears.
A little love, a little care, a little offering; Can't you?
If you can, you are in his cave, his million eyes (grace) on you!

Service is prayer, kindness is love par excellence; After serving his creation for many births, flows his grace. Paths (many ways exist to God like many ways mountain streams take to reach sea) are mere excuses. When time is ripe, lord of lords himself comes with the ladder. All inner forces pave way for freedom! Who has power to stop when he wills to return? His milestones are everywhere but hidden to the little mind.

Have a little patience. Have a little faith. Remain simple. Be kind be genuine. Yes, he does come, and beloved Atman's presence heal all deep wounds. We all cry we all sob in private we all are hungry for morsels of love. But our ego hides the true pain. Death, disease, old age, long wait in womb to see light again, are not new to anyone. At times in deep pain we move like corpses, among the happy ones hiding our faces.

But, in just one glance the longest wait ends. Grace flows when you least expected it, when you return rejected, dejected, depressed and hopeless after trying hard for long. All turn nectarine as his presence overpowers you, as the cosmos which looked external to ego/me again flows back in you, again blooms in you, as your own creation of love.

Maya or the great illusion that fashioned the cosmos is yours (you are the supreme in hide), the trap/avidya/ignorance too is yours, trapped everywhere too is your beloved dream creation. Call it reflected consciousness, call it ego, but truth is, what can happen without your (Brahman) knowing / witnessing / seeing? Who is not yours? Time, space, laws all yours. The great king of kings is paraded in his own kingdom for a little fault (has forgotten who he is, mistaking the shadow as real, forgetting his self).

All cosmos is but one undifferentiable infinite whole. Part is the illusion, whole the truth. Soul is million-fold more blissful than the highest ever pleasure available to beings. Hope sparkles in cloud of despair. Like the peacock dancing in joy with the onset of monsoon, the love thirsty creature that wandered in vain along the unknown terrains of mind, erupts in joy. All barriers open, suddenly you land in the wonderous and magical infinite sky(a brand new sky) ,suddenly you float in ecstasy, suddenly all cosmos look dreamland, moment to moment you turn intoxicated as the flood of consciousness swipe away your little body, you are carried away somewhere you never ever imagined. Death fear lifts. Same cosmos that looked so dull and dreadful, same cosmos where you shed tears look beautiful.

Ramanujan's Vishishtadvaita is a combination of Bahuvyapi aspect and Antarvyapi aspect of truth.

Can tantra be a means to samadhi?

Any object of love can be used as a tool of meditation to take seeker beyond mind, body, and surroundings. Once withdrawn from physical, ego remains in mental plane and if withdrawn from there too, it(ego) dissolves.

Divine Tantra

Any object of intense interest can naturally pull a seeker away from external world   and half work (pratyahara) of yoga is already over;

Now from that very hight, if truely adored with intense bhakti, tremendous curiocity, and truely intimate love coupled with focussed attention to go to the depth or origin of the object, the object dissolves in the subject;   And when both object and subject consciousness dip, infinite bliss flows.

Prema or love is a very potent weapon to land one in the land of super consciousness. Absorbed in intense love for beloved Krishna (Atman), Radha rani is liberated from body.

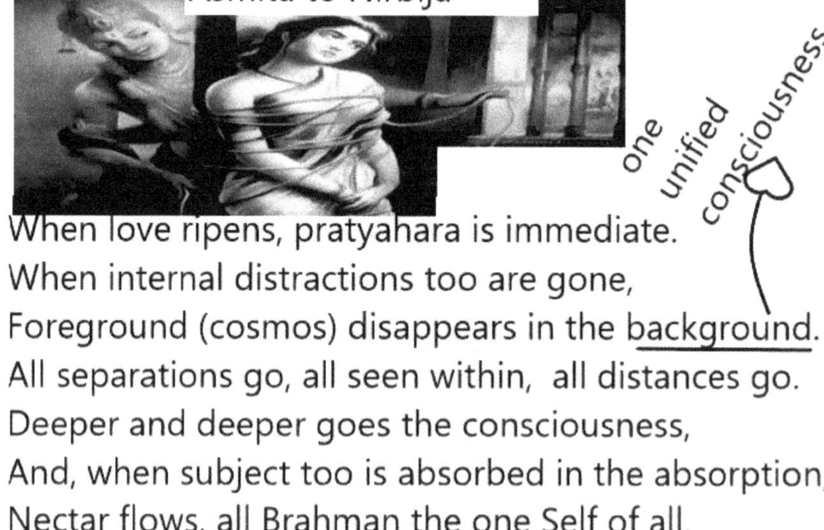

Selfless karma as advised in Mahabharata also opens the door to viswarupa darshan.

Whatever the path is, keep the search on. You never know when you are called back. You never know when the wind of liberation starts to flow. You never know when the lightening tears apart the impregnable dark clouds. Keep travelling. All will go there one day. There is no way oh traveller! There is no other way!

Keep meditating:

Stung early it sought again,

Nothing could hold it long,

Tone of dukkha pulled mind away,

Knocked this temple, that temple in vain,

Hopeless and desperate, corpse like it moved,

Hunger tore it, mocked at it,

A few hesitant steps into Samasara, came a call,

It was Anantha the eternal companion!

Kundalini Yoga:

Another kind of Yoga too works. Seeker goes beyond material worlds through control of Prana.

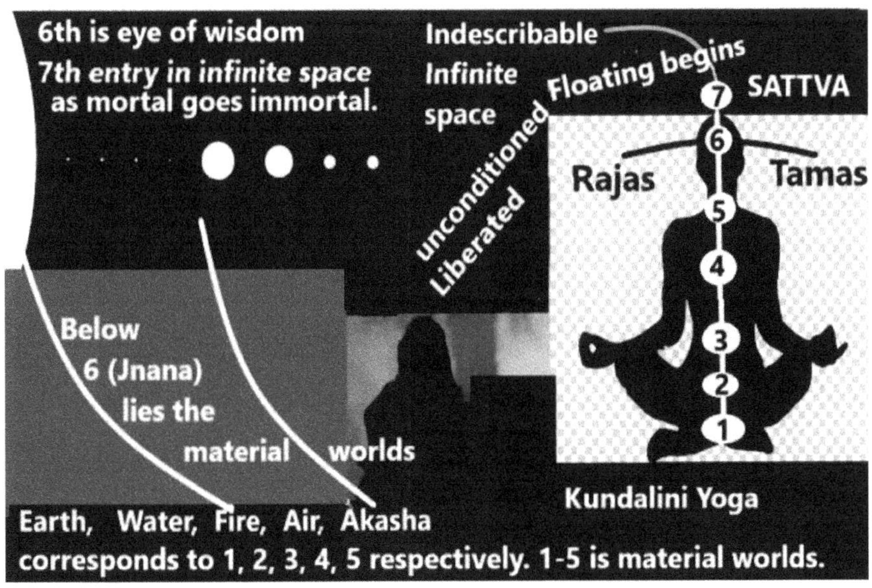

Pratyahara:

No need to wait for right time to begin; Search now; Start now; Pray now. Start withdrawal now. Start it in youth. Who has seen tomorrow? Real pratyahara starts with lifting of the cover of Maya. If pratyahara is full and final dhyana, dharana, samadhi are not far away.

Pratyahara

Withdrawal from worldly engagements and attachments
by reflecting on the transient nature of all things and
experiences. Satsang, simple living, kindness, faith, service help.

As youth wanes,
As one laments in old age,
As disease doesn't leave,
As death howls,
As uncertainty of future torments

As will goes feeble,
As friends die one by one,
As body can't permit desire,
It is hard to meditate.
Still, if you can do.

Pratyahara is beautiful, as stillness speaks the unspoken while taking ego to its svabhava; Thrilling starts, all recalled, as mother nature offers her lap for the one who values pure love.

Reflect on Sufferings in the worlds.

We are migrants in an alien land. Tear flows, mood not there to eat as their plights come to picture. People loot billions. Who cares for them? On their tears are built the tall buildings, on their death bed is built the monuments of love. In hunger they move herded together like cattle. Who cares? And we talk of God! We build masjids, churches, temples and pray God. Nobody is there to take care of their children. Trucks trample million animals. Who cares? Which court is for them? They look with million questions on their faces. They stand resigned to their fates. When juice is squeezed out, they are thrown away like old bullocks. His creation in such pain...

Value not that which would depart one day,
    Value the little light that is within,
    All dreams would fade, all travellers would leave,
    Walk alone naked,
    Walk alone absorbed as a child with mother.
    Your path, your travel, your faith,
    Break not in dukkha, the only light flashing all along.
    If you break not, the immortal path opens.

The battle is ever on between desire for liberation and desire for enjoyment.

You can't break mind by force; Body is in the grab of mind and mind can break it; Give chariot to Krishna and carry out work in a detached manner! Very difficult indeed is Samsara; In a moment weather changes; No need to be a Buddha to see dukkha; Life is a mere bubble, a delicate flower to wither in a moment; Thirst quenched or not who cares? Time devours all.

What are the different Koshas or layers that cover the Atman or Brahman?

Like the recoiling of the tortoise, the seeker must withdraw from the outer to the inner layers. At outer layer noise is more, fight is more. As one turns inward calmness increases. With light asana, pranayama and sattvic food one can easily control the prana and physical layers. With intense reflection on the transient nature of our earthly existence one can rein the mind too. Sudden and forceful practices hardly help. Yoga must be slow and steady. The five koshas are physical or annamaya, pranamaya, manomaya, vijnanamaya and anandamaya. Beyond these layers is the abode of Atman.

What is the message delivered by Krishna to the mankind through Vishwarupa Darshana? Nishkama Karma. We have no hand in the fruit of our actions. Only righteous action with no desire for rewards frees the Jivatma or ego from the vicious cycle of death and birth.

A Buddhist path to liberation by cultivatingenlightenment qualities and purification.Mindfulness: Mindfulness body, feelings, mental states, and mental qualities; **Right** Efforts: Exertion for the preventing of unskilful states to arise, exertion for the abandoning of the already arisen unskilful states, exertion for the arising of skilful states, exertion for the sustaining and increasing of arisen skilful states; Bases of mental power: Will, Energy, Effort, Consciousness, Examination; Spiritual faculties: Conviction, Energy, Effort, Mindfulness, Unification, Wisdom; Strength: Conviction, Energy, Effort, Mindfulness, Unification, Wisdom;Factors of Enlightenment: Mindfulness, Investigation, Energy, Effort, Joy, Tranquillity, Unification, Equanimity; Eightfold Path: Right Understanding, Right Intention, Right Speech, Right Action, Right Livelihood, Right Effort, Right Mindfulness, Right Unification.

Path of purification: Purification of Conduct, Purification of Mind, Purification of View, Purification by Overcoming Doubt; Purification by Knowledge and Vision of What Is Path and Not Path; Purification by Knowledge and Vision of the Course of Practice; Knowledge of contemplation of rise and fall; Knowledge of contemplation of dissolution; Knowledge of appearance as terror;Knowledge of contemplation of danger;;Knowledge of contemplation of dispassion; Knowledge of desire for deliverance;Knowledge of contemplation of reflection; Knowledge of equanimity about formations

CHAPTER SIX

MY JOURNEY

Pull:

It all started with a little sweet pull somewhere couldn't recall.
She pulled to here, He pulled to there,
my boat stuck once again halfway!
Those signals too faint to catch, these signals too magical to believe.
And my broken boat capsized.
Little did I know, it was the wind of liberation brewing within,
Little did I know, this mesmerizing world was being snatched away!

Departing days: In the last couple of births after maya is partially lifted and before Nirvikalpa, Jiva intensely recalls its stays in samsara and wonders "In fear I missed the depth and beauty of this magnificent creation in full". One recalls how and where the path to home was lost. Memory of past lives flashes as all fear lifts. One gets infinitely connected to the fabric of creation. Joy unbounded keeps it inebriated. The eternal fragrance of union absorbs mind from morning to night. Seasons come and go but the mind hardly returns to gross. For a while, the fragile windows of senses keep bringing sweet foods. The same ego sits in a corner lamenting, no longer interested in the morsels thrown at it. The eternal has dealt the lethal blows. An actor is leaving the show from the theatre of Maya.

> Q: When did I see you in full?
> A: When did you wait to see?
>
> **Maya & Brahman**
>
> Q: Was there ever any respite from fear to stand and stare?
> A: Was it so from beginning?
> Q: Can't recall my beginning; Can't recall
>   who put shackles around my feet;
>   Can't recall who ordered them; Can't
>   recall who deluded me; Can't recall
>   who I really I am.
> A: Wait awhile and see who began it all!
>
> **Aware**
> **Living**
> **Whose Maya?**
> **Whose creation?**

The Search:
> The little traveller (ego) comes,
> Opens baggage (body), roams in city (mind),
> Purchases things,makes friends,makes enemies,sings,dances,
> Time flies, baggage grows heavy, old, and painful to carry,
> Friend's part ways, cold night, road desolate,
> Laments and repents, hurries to safety,
> Worse still, baggage snatched away,
> Cries, nobody there to listen,
> Pits head on ground (own karma), searches new,
> Moves on, howls all around,
> Past graveyard, a little light flash!
> Somebody (parents) calls in,
> Moves (rebirth) to another city.

Tired of city after city, graveyard after graveyard,
Tired of baggage after baggage,
Ponders what it is doing, where it is, why it is here.
And the search begins.

The early life among nature: Father was a primary school teacher in a remote village of Keonjhar district of Odisha state. We were seven brothers and sisters staying in a little government quarter. Mother was always ill. Father was busy keeping the noble job which was the only source of income.

There was a small stream flowing in gay abandon a few hundred meters behind our quarter. In that stream I fished with my elder brother from morning to afternoon with scant regard for school hours. Hours passed without notice till hunger reminded to return. With a few tiny fishes woven in a grass root we marched back to home with great pride. We discussed the great skills we applied to conquer their freedom. We measured their sizes, weights and discussed their shapes and colours with great delight. We lamented over the missed chances. Several fishes outwitted us, foiled all our tricks. There was only one fishing rod which was used by my brother. I simply assisted him improving my skill each day with the expert. The fishing rod was a great asset kept in a secret place lest angry father should throw it away.

Early rain filled us with great hope as surviving fishes from last summer rose anew from holes partaking in birth of a fresh fish empire. Each day we valued the chances of resuming our fishing journey. Each day the size, number, and variety of fishes were judged with great effort. The rod was repaired soon. The stage was laid. The earth worms which served as bait were located. And the fishing fair started once again. Two tiny figures were seen with a rod on the little stones on the bank of the meandering stream. The bait was firmly fixed in a bush and the catch began in the gushing water in the unruly stream. It was a great engagement with pristine nature. Attachment to nature was very intense; We responded and jumped in joy when stones, trees, streams called us every morning. Heart and soul mingled in the lap of nature. Struggle for food, dress and shelter was intense. But we never felt the dire poverty we were thrown into, due to constant and intense love of nature. **Nature is a great healer.**

Me unaware yet, nature had started sharing her inner journey. Her tale is deep; She had picked this little kid. Her spell was on. She whispered her secrets. Little did I know, she was mine; Little did I know she was eager to unite after ages! Great messages exchanged between us two, me unaware!

She whispered "I am in you! Hold me there. Don't let me come out. Don't let me separate. Let this birth be your last here!".

Nature is the bridge to eternity; Live in harmony with her; Don't let her bleed by our greed; When she bleeds, can her kids stay unharmed? The fabric or substratum or infinite space is but one and any panic or love wave anywhere has far reaching repercussions everywhere. We are entangled at a cosmic scale, each of our action influences the whole fabric, name it karma, name it particle entanglement, name it whatever; We are one here externally and internally, and we go there as one as well.

"Look deep into nature, and then you will understand everything better." - Albert Einstein

Still remember, how rainwater trickled down through the broken roof tiles, wetting the little living room. We put kadhai, tawa, glass etc. wherever water struck the floor to get rid of cold water splashing against our half-torn bed sheets. There was no mat. There was no bed. The sound of the thunder and the flashes of the lightening coupled with the chill wind of winter at times mocked at us. But we never felt the pain. We enjoyed the dance of raw nature to the full. There was no electricity. The kerosene lamp would smear the walls. The bed bugs constantly woke us in the depth of night. Nature was enjoyed to the full and there was no planning except the dream for fishing and capturing birds. **Freedom was at its peak; joy was at its peak despite physical discomforts.**

We spent lots of time watering vegetable and flower plants. In cold foggy mornings as we jumped in our treasure groves, the sparkling pearl drops on cabbage leaves was a feast to our eyes. Mind danced among bees and butterflies while the divine painter was busy filling sky for another grand show. The light arrangement in the firmament had started, the stage was being reset. Nature was inviting audience from far and near for another show. Lesser actors (birds) were hopping and chirping around as well. Nobody wanted to be left behind. The corner karabira and madhumalati flowers swaying in morning breeze were inviting us to a different land as we nestled around them.

The bullock cart carrying dried cow dungs was coming out of Ramesh's (a neighbour) cowshed. They were heading for the distant paddy fields with manures. The whistles and beating of the unruly bullocks were audible to us. They disappeared into another world.

Thick smokes and known smells from our grand kitchen reminded us of our important morning duty. In hardly two to three minutes tooths were brushed with tooth sticks gathered from back side fence. Elder sister had started preparing the same menu unasked. All custard apples in the back side of our quarter were rechecked one by one for ripeness. They were not many. Rather, hands out numbered them. All the famous hide outs and bushes for berries were rescanned with great skill! We had allowed (while we were asleep) them around half day of freedom! **We valued all.** We wasted nothing. We had no choice, but we never felt restricted! We had great freedom! The message is, in accepting what god has given lies great peace! **We resist and build walls of separation and cry!**

Slowly, figures tall and short, bulky, and lean pushing fog away ran hither and thither. The village road near the old banyan tree was bustling again with new hopes of a new day. Once again activities around the school's water well had picked up in full swing. It was the only well in that big village. The well was very deep, the circumference was big. In its stone holes down lived many old sparrows. Despite all manoeuvres, I was unable to catch even a single sparrow. That well was a big mystery for me. I circled around the well with great pride as if I owned it. For no obvious reason, I felt as if my privacy was breached, and people had no regards for my silent order.

To continue the morning tale, village women poured water into their earthen pitchers placed all around the well. I often wondered how they were recognizing each other's assets. As water hurled out at the pitchers from the less adept ones missed the narrow tops and splashed and spilled all over, morning sun mixed red colour in them. It was a delight for me. Each had a story to tell. Several threads of discussions charged the air. I had no interest, and I left the spot.

In a corner mother was heating her hands and legs in the little fire lit with dried leaves saved with great care. Another show in the theatre of Maya had already begun. In short, we were absorbed by external nature throughout days be it summer, be it spring, be it dusk, be it morning. Life was full. We lacked nothing. We had no big plan. The message is **we buy worries with our greed!**

The nearby pond with a lonely mahua tree served our only reservoir. The bank of the pond was very slippery, and the tiny feet made several trips to that pond to see the rising water after every fresh spell of rain. After every spell of rain, the stream down sucked water flowing from paddy fields on both sides; Swollen up in pride It overflowed its banks and frightened the creatures around with its noise; Visible from our quarter window, it was constantly calling us to its lap. The life was live.

Early college days: Decades ago, it was a very sweet phase of life among rising hopes of gathering new foods and barricading the nest. It was 'me and my family' versus. rest of the world; We were lost among things; We enjoyed separation from him; We hardly believed when elders shouted to bow down at his lotus feet! Blood was warm, flesh was shining, spring was everywhere. I was studying in SCS college, Puri. And there in his temple precinct we spent evenings after evenings discussing earthly matters; We never saw him there; We were lost in our little world of things. The evening breeze, the sea shore, the early morning chant in temple are unforgettable. We used to wake up to a warm welcome from the Temple.

शुक्लाम्बरधरं विष्णुं शशिवर्णं चतुर्भुजम् । प्रसन्नवदनं ध्यायेत् सर्वविघ्नोपशान्तये ॥

The four (north, south, east, west) temple doors closing one by one from inside; Who else left outside to close otherwise? You and me alone; What is left in cosmos to return to? All mere shadows of you; Your irresistible pull, your fragrance, your fragrant walls with monkeys and birds, your radiant lamps, your flower bed, your prasad, the voice of your dear devotees, your infinite eyes, your arti, your brother and sister all allure me; They all call me; They all absorb me; I am in your abode again in body and mind, O my beloved prabhu Jagannath, my आराध्य देवता ; I offer myself to you! Be with me, be with me.

Now same world is folded,ind is folded; Time and space are folded; The eternal chariot is waiting; World is a sweet memory, whether within or without, whether far or near, whether sweet or sour. Don't know, how many hours left of this shadow; Packing is over; Journey is ending!!

First escape (the height of intoxication): Two times I tried to escape samsara from college hostel. First attempt was on December 6th, 1987, when I was in first semester. Filled with tear, inebriated with desire for truth I headed to the Rourkela railway station penniless and without any winter wear. With a slipper and worn-out shirt, I boarded a train without ticket.

A close friend (Baroda Mishra) had cycled me all the way to the railway station. He was a skeleton then; How he pedalled me up the hilly road to the station couldn't imagine. He was the electrical branch topper, our electrical guru and master of electron, at least so we thought of him then. We mercilessly preached to him, and he giggled, never uttering a word of protest. His only words were "So what?". Don't recall what thought flowed from hostel to railway station; Don't recall how he responded to my questions; Don't recall how he agreed to my plan for escape; Many thanks to him who served unknowingly as a very vital link. Without his help that day, I couldn't have been able to escape so easily.

We reached the station. It was around noon. Mind was completely intoxicated with God; Such was the urgency that I couldn't wait even a minute more; Don't recall what parting words exchanged between me and Baroda; Tear was nonstop rolling out of the eyes. As If the train was taking me directly to him, as if it was the last and only train, I hurried towards the train which was already standing with the thought "It's God's train, it's God's world, it's God everywhere. Why worry? He would take care"; It was general class compartment and can't recall whether I got a seat or travelled standing. It was the height of meditation.

Little did I imagine, right from hostel to Banaras it was a long spell of samadhi. **I was already in what I was after.** We are blind. I never had a chance to read the scriptures. Only a few books from Swami Vivekanada and Swami Yogananda had inspired me. My room was reverberating with day night discussions of hollow nature of atom and the mysterious laws of science. Appetite for divine union was on rise. The fever was on.

Coming back to the journey, the ticket collector came, asked about the ticket, and surprisingly went to the next cabin. Somebody called him exactly when he was asking me about the ticket and never returned. I had no fear. Drenched in an unknown current of love flowed almost unaware for more than a thousand kilometres. There was intense joy when train was speeding past the dilapidated Buddhist structures of Bodh Gaya on left side." Buddham Saranam Gacchami" was vibrating in mind. Mind was gathered and one pointed around the joy of meeting the unknown.

Still can't recall what prompted me to get down in Banaras. Banaras could have been the last station for that train. In Banaras railway station a rikshaw took me into the heart of the holy city. Don't recall why he took me, how he took me, where he took me. But I met a man who asked "Son, your family is in great distress. Go back home". I was in tear asking, "Will I ever see god this life". He told "Yes". He asked "What have you taken son? " . He then sent someone for Jilebi (a sweet) and told "Son. You are hungry. Take these laddu first." Now as I recall, I wonder who that person was, where that person was, why I went to that unknown person as if we had known each other for decades. With great intimacy we exchanged some words for a couple of hours. My eyes were constantly on the lord Hunuman's photo hanging on the wall. He was looking like a homeopath. And as I recall I know he was some divine messenger. And many such things happened till I descended from the inebriated state and as soon as I descended sufferings returned. I trembled in winter chill with nothing to eat, waiting for the unknown journey. Yes, it was my first escape in vain. But the brewing of the divine intoxication had begun.

Meditation practice: Heart throbs as I recall those golden days of tryst with destiny in the backyard of pristine nature. We daily escaped hostel with a big mug in hand along the dusty hill tracks till we disappeared in the sylvan surroundings. We used to fetch milk right from the cowsheds located a kilometre or so away from our campus. In night, tired of asanas and intense reflection, sleep often overpowered right in the evening. Don't recall who used to wake me up for dinner. Many times, dinner was asked to room. This privilege was exercised at the slightest pretext. Many times, dinner was missed altogether. I still remember how I hurried to kitchen when the kitchen was about to close and was glad to get whatever food was left. It was raw hunger for food and truth coupled together. My life was a complete mesh. I was completely dirty, obstinate, absent minded and undisciplined since childhood. Nature had absorbed my soul. Science never appealed to me although I had opted it out of hunger for a job.

Dozens of times as soon as sleep came one dream repeatedly hounded me "My examination form is not filled. And there is no chance. One year is wasted". This recurring dream was from my previous lives. I had many births lost in vain searching truth. After a few instances of deep logical analysis, "Rebirth is certain" became a fact. I no more had to recall.

Things gathered momentum in spiritual front and academics was relegated to background. Marks in examinations were horribly low. College attendance was low. College Lab classes were missed. Search for truth overshadowed all other activities. Yet, the efforts were unorganised, hap hazard and impulsive. We were experts in Padmasana, Sarvangasana, Halasana, Chakrasana, Mayurasana etc. and there was no scheduled time and fixed duration for them. All asanas were done with utmost precision. Wherever and whenever mind asked asana started, lecture started. Don't recall how other friends treated us. I must have been an unsocial fellow in the eyes of hostel mates without doubt.

The storm: The perennial questions "Who am I? Where am I? Why am I here? Since when I am here? Who are they? What is this world? Who created and why? Why are there sufferings? What am I doing here? Is there any ray of hope? Where should I begin my search?" kept hounding me throughout the day unsettling me, sending fear waves through my spine. The incessant fear of loss of youth, disease and death stared at me testing my nerve. The storm was brewing me unaware of it. With much effort the academic works were performed whenever got a little break to look at the body. Dress was unkempt, skin was uncared, mind was elsewhere. The great hunt had long begun. Both hungers were at logger heads tearing me into pieces. Vairagya was raging all over, overthrowing my little existence. The little leaf was too feeble to resist the whirlpools of individual pralaya. Yes, it was reflection on dukkha that absorbed me. Although, then I was unaware what had absorbed me.

Nature: Trees, sun, moon, cloud, forest, streams kept me alive. I often breathed a sigh of deep relief in the proximity of raw nature. The ambience of the college was a paradise for me. The banyan trees in front of the hostel, the golden leaves of the tall Saal trees swirling in air and reaching me, the little pond behind, the trees within the compound all colluded to take me afar into the mystical world to finish my earthly existence. The storm of liberation that had started in previous lives kept passing again over this birth uprooting my little world of clay. My little dolls were vehemently snatched away, me not able to decode the hidden messages. The storm of liberation was everywhere.

Rooms: I often recall two old pictures hanging on our room walls. One was a very dark-complexioned photo of Mother Kali with a terrific tongue protruding out of her mouth, standing on the back of lord Shiva. The other was a hatha yoga chart. The Jnana yoga book of Swami Vivekananda was a pampered treasure with its important pages folded, excessively underlined, and smeared with dirty fingers. I can't recall what happened to that book in course of our great spiritual conquest. I missed that priceless treasure somewhere. I recall the pages I straightway jumped into when something clicked my mind in the depth of night. They ignited the fire and kept it alive.

Our temple: I recall how impatient we were to escape to the hills to resume our search. Once we returned from college, in a few minutes we were back on the backside hillocks. We jumped from stone to stone and discussed under the setting sun. We discussed like seasoned scholars unaware of what destiny had in store for us. We were hardly aware what we were doing, where we were heading to. The great impetus was on, and the fierce fight was raging in the inner world without our notice. The transformation was on. The raw fight was at height.

Time: Decades after, I recall the same little rock where we meditated lying buried in memory; Those days it was separate from me lying outside, now it is inside; All separations gone; It springs up only when I recall; It is neither inside nor outside when I don't; Time too has passed by only when I recall; There is nothing called time as such If I don't recall; I am beyond time and space; I am the Atman; I am within this world; I am beyond;

Early morning: Around 3 o'clock we woke up in morning. As the front gate of the hostel was still locked from inside, after a brisk bath we escaped through the back gate to the nearby hills. There we meditated till at around 7:30 AM we were reminded of returning to hostel by the sound of the cowherd boys. Baked in early sun and in the same dress we took some tiffin and ran to the college. Where was the time to check the time table? After lot of labour, we had secured a seat in the college. And unaware we were spoiling our chances of a decent academic career. We came so close to a great career yet went so far.

Guru: I still remember how I bribed my only wristwatch to a baba who I adored for no special reason. Anybody, anything that promised us of connecting to God was adored and anything that reminded us of academics was a thing of hate. Time rolled on and divinity looked far. Yet we were optimistic.

Second escape: Again, we (with Ramesh Mallick) escaped to Ajodhya in second year without any success. It was late spring and early summer. The raw charm of season was at its peak. It was totally unplanned like the first escape. At the destination, after alighting from train we walked down from the track and by the side road headed to a small village. We were delighted to find a few bearded sadhus in ochre robes along our walk. Probably their sight was the only noteworthy event. We had imagined a lot but were disappointed with what we got. We visited lord Ram's temple on a very raised platform, and after offering our obeisance loitered here and there without any plan. After a day or so, when emotions got exhausted recalled our college. And with failure written large over the face we rushed back ashamed. We had no face to show. When we returned, it was noon time and in scorching sun we headed to take bath. It was general class journey up and down for thousands of kilometres with scant food and sleep. Body was needing rest. Smell of jack fruit was coming from the next room. Somebody had plucked a ripe jackfruit from the hostel trees. With some food in belly, we threw our bodies on bed as if two great warriors had returned from a big war.

Our bodies were seasoned with Asanas and Pranayama. We were self-styled yoga experts. And the journey continued. The stubborn mind never left hope. Attempt after attempt were going in vain. Constant effort to realize truth was on wherever whenever condition was a little conducive to meditation. Among ups and downs life flowed. And the college days passed like hours absorbed in meditation.

The fall: Around 6th semester pushed back by nature, mind returned to regather the lost academics to manage the great show of 'doing engineering from a premier college'. But it was too little too late. The career was irreparably damaged. With great effort managed to secure a first class. What would have been a cake walk looked like an Aegean stable. And under the pressure of expectation life became a burden. The joy and warmth were missing. And a bitter phase of life was staring at me in utter disdain.

Work life: The thought on the four-fold miseries kept coming right from childhood and after every spell of happiness there was a pause. The fear of death and loss of youth never allowed to settle mind on any material engagement for long. There was no immediate reason for the fear. Health was good. But spontaneously the fear loomed over me. I kept reflecting on the creation whenever mind didn't force me to material desire. At times material hunger was irrepressible and like a dry leaf in a whirl wind the mind was engrossed in material enjoyment. I was extremely emotional. There was extreme attachment to nature. I recall how I desperately struggled to have a glance of moon when walking in the crowded lanes of Mumbai. As if in the dean and bustle of modern life the Atman was lost somewhere. Terrible pain filled the days and almost like a corpse moved the little body. Material desire interspersed with spiritual desire and the life was indescribable. Neither was steadfast in yoga nor in work. The search for eternal life was continuous yet, the force in effort was missing. Terrible material hunger blinded me sometimes and the practice of asana, pranayama was not systematic. The rigorous hatha yoga practice in the graduation was missing. Thirst of belly was overpowering the thirst for realization. Chill penury was suppressing noble thoughts. Friend circle was a few. Family had pinned a great hope on me. But I was not able to deliver. Pain predominantly marked the days. It looked an uphill task to control the mind as asked by Arjuna to beloved Krishna in the battlefield of Mahabharat. Bhagavad Gita:

chanchalam hi manah krishna pramathi balavad dridham
tasyaham nigraham manye vayor iva su-dushkaram

Food: After many futile efforts spanning decades was finally able to get rid of the habit of tobacco and nonveg. The effect of yoga started bearing fruit once I got rid of them.

The re-entry: The entry in infinite space signals the beginning of realization. It starts with floating what day what night. The farther one expands the fainter goes the things. It is liberating. It is wonder of wonders. Buried under responsibilities I had almost forgotten for decades that I ever had searched truth. In utter hopelessness and despair, I had returned empty handed. The fire was still there buried deep within. It was September 2018. It was Bangalore. As I woke up from sleep, I couldn't believe my eyes. All looked like moving shadows. I first touched the wardrobe, then looked at my kid, all looked so different, all looked so unreal. It was neither dream, nor awake, nor deep sleep. Next, I saw the building floating, then the city too. All roads started to float. I had to leave for office. Didn't tell anybody anything about it. I was wondering "I am going mad. What is it happening to me? What will happen to my little world?". Yet, there was a deep sense of relief and the long choked spirit had tasted the fragrance of the wild. All things near and far were melting, rising, sinking and flowing in Me. I boarded the bus. And to my surprise the bus was flowing in Me. Somehow located the office in Bharatiya city. And the office too started flowing in me swimming like a fish in water. I tried to apply all my wits to decipher the new experience. No science worked. How could things float without liquid? Then, I realized "All world is in my mind, and I had entered the Manomaya Kosha." And the jubilation began. I was in infinite space of consciousness. The fluid like substance in which all melted and started floating was the fluid of infinite space the ethereal substance that long defied science. Oh! It was the absolute frame of reference. And I was far past the speed of light in an alien land.

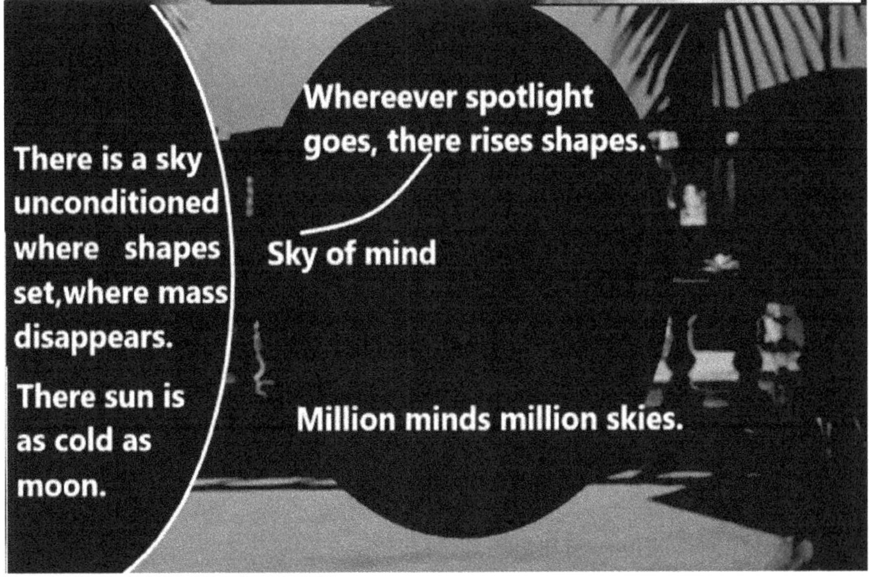

Worldly signals rarely reach there; Guru too is rare; Some golden clues buried somewhere help.

Worldly signals can't reach there;   Some rare words buried in pages (by some great soul's own journey) of time connect.

A guru there is rare to find when in dire need;All alone, all within,   riding the transcendental waves;

The boat at times slows down,   subconscious monsters frighten.
Will outwits all.

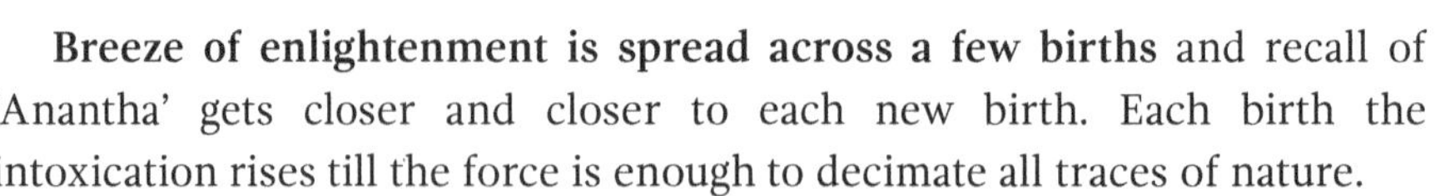

Breeze of enlightenment is spread across a few births and recall of 'Anantha' gets closer and closer to each new birth. Each birth the intoxication rises till the force is enough to decimate all traces of nature.

Sufferings: The last few births are very painful as the friction between subconscious inner nature and the indomitable urge for freedom rises. Mind too has seen the lord in the last birth but has forgotten. Senses are still in darkness like the unruly child trying to put its finger on fire.

Enlightenment is not mere counting beads. **It's the fiercest battle ever.** There is a price to everything. Maya doesn't lift so easily. It is cleaning inner field and uprooting trees of desires. It is declaring inner war against senses and mind. The retaliation often brings death to many seekers, and they perish in the caves unnoticed. But the effort is not wasted. Yes, if you are fortunate to be in contact with an enlightened guru, then you are steered clear of many hurdles.

The very normal feelings and state we neglect so often look rare and special during days of deep depression. In the corpse like state, one almost forgets that 'normal happiness is ever possible again'. Suffering or passing these days of deep depression helplessly sows the seed of intense desire for liberation. When one's existence is threatened by Maya, one questions lord 'Why this? How long this? Is there no way out?'. Each day looks like a year, seasons come and go, but there is no good news.

World moves on with myriad colours, while the corpse like body is dragged laboriously. All colours fade. One hides one's face from others. One gets suffocated beyond toleration. One still takes the feeble steps holding on to the fading dream, hoping against hope that eternal can return. These days burn the seed of samsara. Each moment looks like a death moment. Holding on to the nerve in these trying situations clinches the game in favour.

One is so much stressed that neither normal nor fearful dream come in sleep. Terrible, very terrible are these days; Tear no more flows; Pain becomes chronic; Dark night, dark days, dark evenings, and the war continues. Each drop of fresh rain reminding sweet memory of past pains, each moment of happiness brings pain. Body and mind are out of sync. If one is to get enlightenment, no doctor should be consulted these days, and deep prayer is the only ray of hope. Drugs are temporary solution that can bring one out, but the golden messages are lost. If one endures with reflection, the lightning strikes. Anantha flashes!

First entry to the zone of nectar can happen anywhere may be on earth, maybe on heaven. This entry is allegorically referred to as sighting Brahman Jyoti. Lord buddha called it stream entry. Experience is same. One lands in infinite space. This infinite space is unconditioned and unaffected by whims of mind. Whole subtle creation seen from this infinite space. And, coincident with floating in infinite space an infinite pull slightly similar to 'entry into deep sleep' takes ones 'chetana' afar. This बेहोश is completely different from normal बेहोश state. Its entry into a superconscious plane and all संज्ञा gone, all markers gone, all cognition gone, only little traces of avidya remains. Each time one descends one recalls it was with truth. Each time one connects, there is no traces of time and space.

In rare cases one enters the ultimate gate, the gate of nectar becoming that (referred to as Brahman and this is pure nectar with no subject, object and perception). There are trillions of earth like planets and this very moment countless new galaxies and fresh creations are happening. Why only Sumeru? Why only earth? Creation is centreless, horizon less and magical. Is there a limit on magic? Why lament for this scar on this dot oh dear? You are Anantha. Same pathetic field of ego turns nectarine. Whatever you touch turns gold one day.Inebriated you leave this little body one day.

Inner Mahabharat: The game of eternal freedom is not easy. Win is at end when darkness almost bends the spine. Decades of depression continues when fight between vivek and body seems unending. Dukkha looms large. This is the trying hours. If fought with conviction and faith, victory is snatched from jaws of death! With steely nerve maya is counter attacked!

I recall a rare experience that happened three decades ago on the hillock at the back gate of my hostel. After a cycle journey of 30 kms body was very tired and throwing the cycle in hostel we as usual rushed to the hill. Body was laid on a little rock, eyes were transfixed on the celestial show staged in the distant sky. Apart from the faint murmur of the little stream down it was silence all over. The full moon was challenging the ego to leave the body and adore her deeper and deeper. The body consciousness was slipping away. Senses were bemused. Inner nature had reconnected to the source. The cloud was kissing the face of the moon which briskly ran away afar. The stage was enough for the hungry spirit to come out of its nest. Suddenly I was exported to a state of bliss. My friend (Ramesh Mallick) was resting beside me. Could not recall how much time passed in that state. There was no me to record as the divine union was on. Don't recall how I separated and landed back on the stone. As body consciousness came back, I came back dancing to another close friend's (Nirakara) room. He was as sweet as ever with a very infectious smile beaming on his face. He was a very high order devotee. It was the first taste of Nirvikalpa. There was no subject, no object, no experience. The blast of bliss had engulfed all. There is no opulence on earth to match that. It far outshone all material and mental pleasures. It stands out clear and loud among all other mortal experiences.

Vairagi's inner desire doesn't go in vain. Golden dusk nears. Samadhi comes. As ascension starts, transition time view of universe from eye of wisdom is strange. Old cosmos where it built nests all get flooded by consciousness, cosmos turns a dream land floating within.

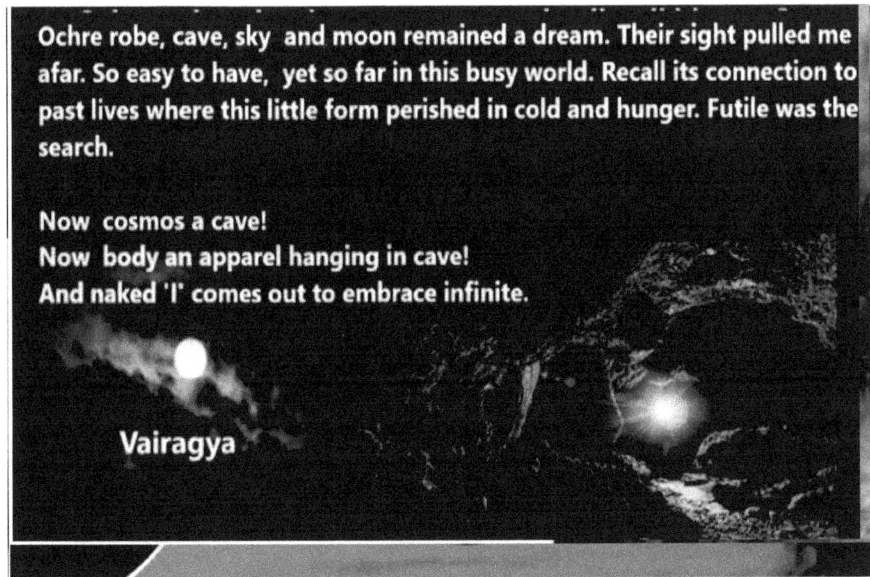

As the Atman strikes in the thick cloud of despair, the same cosmos looks strange!

Eternal life returns. Further meditation continues in dream land or mental land. The little body mechanically walks as long as prana vibrates, but mind surpassed the gate. Nothing remains to connect, except repeatedly entering the whirlpool of Samadhi. Love of world shifts to Love the Atman. Unknowingly, across lives all mortals wait for that moment; That Anatha prema pulls all; All else are mere acting's under prakriti. Time comes; Whole cosmos turns dream; His little boat sinks in love. This world doesn't even compare to a shadow!! This me is beyond 5 sheaths and disappears leaving these 5 sheaths as if it never recognized them. And it descends like an eagle to Samsara along the trail of desire. It is a highly lofty state. Death a mere wrong perception dies. You are the immortal canvas of the canvas (Maya). Cosmos is painted on Maya. As time, space, events, and things are seen as perceptions what is the use of magic? All **siddhis** look pale before the Atman.

On way to the pathless, all heavens are crossed. Heavens are mere mental states like this very world we all live in. All magical sciences are intuitively realized and thrown away as garbage. Sun no more burns. Seeker feels the sensations of universes and all laws of cosmos no longer can bind him. Death fear lifts, intoxication rises, one is back in absolute freedom, cosmos unfolds its true colour, light of wisdom more powerful than millions of lightning strike the cloud of despair, the firmament is ablaze with intuition, all horizons look small. Seeker is now whole and complete.

An intermediate state too is briefly experienced. Expanded consciousness spreads as Virata (experiencing cosmos as its body). As mind's periphery is about to be transcended all heavenly states are transcended. People in higher heavens also transcend the mind and the path from earth merge with those paths. As Brahman Jyoti (infinite consciousness) impregnates Brahman Vihara (inner infinite space) cosmos is born. "Seeing" is the distance between seer and seen. As infinite consciousness sees infinite space, illusion (painting called cosmos) is filtered out as impurity. As intimacy between the two develops, impurity or thought decreases and both converge in Nirvikapa as nectar.

Which fool will chase images? Magic is for child who still loves dolls and showing dolls to his friends. When is whole cosmos seen as a mirage which seeker would run after things? And seeing the world as the mirage is wisdom. Some different views of creation are briefly noted here.

world is real	objective reality	*Before Samadhi*	shristi-dristi vada
world is a dream	subjective reality	*Samadhi*	dristi-shristi vada
Like deep sleep and beyond	beyond both	*Within*	ajata vada
			Nirvikalpa Nectar

The realization view is slightly different from these conventional views/vada.
Let us take shristi-dristi as "causal shristi remains even when not observed".
Let us take dristi-shristi as "mental and physical spring from causal as observed ".
Let ajata remains as is as "beyond even appearance and appearance maker".

Seeing highways flowing in infinity while riding vehicle during Samadhi' is a very special experience. All cosmoses seen afloat within. All travels turn internal, be it to far distant galaxy, be it to nearby things. Whole cosmos turns dream. Next, is Ajata, as million flood gates of nectar, sweep ego away.

Acceptance of Viveka is love. Dukkha does exist due to ignorance. We must try to bring harmony in the creation. It helps in meditation. Fight for luxury and dominance over external nature keep us entangled deeply in the net. Simplify living, realign objectives, and keep praying while cutting the wings of Maya with swords of reflection. Respect Rama, Krishna, Jesus, Buddha, Allah, and other saints. They are the same Atman in different names. Power of pardoning others and toleration are great powers. Let true compassion prevails. Let universal brotherhood prevails. Let the cloud of darkness disperse by light. Om Shanthi! Om Shanthi! Let all creatures all over cosmos pray for world peace which should be the highest dharma. India must engage all its age-old values and be the torch bearer in the mission for universal peace and tolerance. Let heart of Buddha and Intellect of Adi Shankara and self-enquiry of Ramana reunite all in the ocean of consciousness. By hurting others, we hurt ourselves.

Harmony with nature: Insensitivity to nature closes the door of wisdom. Sufferings look more fearsome due to lack of rhythm with nature. Nature has key to truth; Fight not with her; Read her messages written in sufferings; Dilution of pain is dilution of pleasure; She bleeds and the kid bleeds; Misuse of body invites disease; Overriding viveka invites pain; Truth is not opposed to nature; Truth is not opposed to science.

CHAPTER SEVEN

SONGS OF SAMADHI

What is Samadhi or Realization? It is impossible to describe samadhi as it starts, progresses and culminates. Many myths are broken. Yet, some sweet memory of the divine union remains after descent. Yes, I am still alive, maybe it is his order to pass on his grace or prasad to posterity!

Pardon me O Lord for any mistakes! It fills this beggar with immense gratitude and love as these feeble fingers muster courage to put down to these pages our marvellous spells of union; It overwhelms this mortal as this awestruck little Ahamkara evades the age-old trap of your Maya and races with infinite speed to embrace you my beloved Atman! I am with you; I am away from you; Our dance is the dance of whole creation. Your beautiful creation seethes in pain separated from you! Million salutes again and again O my beloved! With utmost humility and surrender this little creature is trying to bring your messages for your creation!

The dance of liberation doesn't finish in one spell. The spell is cast on the arrogant me and the snake or Aham becomes mad in divine ecstasy and eternal love. The flow of divine love engulfs whole creation dissolving all material and immaterial elements. The being is charged with eternal life and in utter wonder passes the remaining days or births in the sky of union. Spells of samadhi gradually become frequent. All remaining stains of mind and body are dropped slowly. The being is healed to the core. The dirt gathered through ignorance spanning numerous lives are purged. The lotus blooms, fragrance spreads and the battlefields where ego fought looks desolate. Silence and solitude prevail. There remains no one except the eternal companion and the dying ego.

Senses bring food but ego is hardly interested. The news of creation no more interests. Whole prakriti with its myriad dance stands silent. No noise or resistance remains. All turn one whole. Million books can't describe union as the inexorable flood of nectar take ego afar to the lap of truth. Truth is revealed. All acting stops. All hunger gets satiated. This very world that tormented the Jiva turns mesmerising. The stone speaks, the idols smile, the inner temple of consciousness calls the beggar ego inside. The periphery of consciousness expands infinitely, threatening the existence of little ego or centre. Atman is everywhere. The Mahavakyas of the mighty Vedas make sense. The creation makes sense; Purpose of creation realized. One no longer complains of the injustice in this world as truth is revealed. **One sees who is behind all.**

Samadhi is the mesmerizing expansion of I-consciousness into pure infinite consciousness as maya lifts. As expansion begins, one instantly connects to the priceless treasure behind this ephemeral creation. Death becomes irrelevant as time, space and causation are transcended. All forces and laws of creation are seen as illusive. The intriguing mind is caught in flight projecting the surroundings around us. All cosmoses come running within with infinite speed. Sun is just a shadow. Nothing remains beyond as Jivatma embraces Paramatma.

Pull:
No waning, no mourning, no death.
I am immortal youth; I am immortal love.
I am silence beyond mind; I am infinite;
I am the source; I am the middle; I am the destination.

Samadhi background: With all humility I can say, be it Sahaja samadhi (throughout day, effortlessly absorbed in infinite while still transacting with material world, a master's eye view) of Ramana Maharshi, be it Sabija (meditating on an object to start with) or Nirbija or Dharma megha of sage Patanjali, be it sunya (all phenomena or dharmas are empty of svabhava) samadhi, be it any other type of samadhi, the taste of samadhi must be same; The rasa or nectar must be same; It hardly matters who got it, where and how. The pratyaya (focussing on an object of interest till object is dissolved in concentrated mind) method, or the various mindfulness methods, or Kriya yoga (union of finite with infinite), or Laya yoga, or Tantra sadhana, or Bhakti bhava, or Nishakama (without desiring fruit of action) Karma yoga, or Prema (path of love), or Jnana marga, or noble Eight-fold path from lord Buddha, or whatever, all must help the meditator bloom into the same truth. All methods and practices directly or indirectly guide the meditator on how to withdraw mind and senses from external or mental things, how to gather, concentrate, and condense the scattered thoughts around a point of deep reflection, and finally dropping the observer or I-ness. Whether we begin with an object used as a rope to climb to truth, or we begin with intense reflection on sufferings, objective is same; Do whatever, but be what you really are. We want perennial freedom from all kinds of fear, be it death, be it disease, be it aging, be it whatever; We want our thirsts to be quenched for ever fed by bliss; We want a permanent solution to our problems; We want silence, inner peace, harmony and love; We want to be eternally existent, intimately connected, and complete; We seek absolute and eternal freedom from all pangs of separations; We want union or yoga with our real Self.

Samadhi is a broad spectrum of expanding consciousness; Samadhi is generally considered as a meditative absorption of individual soul in the supreme soul or paramatma or Brahman. Samadhi is a very very deep topic; Primary view points we can consider are the eight spheres or planes of dhyanas (four Rupa dhyanas and four Arupa dhyanas) of lord Buddha, and the ten types of samadhi mentioned in the "Yoga Sutras" from the great sage Patanjali. But, experience (or beyond experience) in summary is, "All cosmos seen afloat in the expanded Me!, and the still deeper one that takes away all external and physical consciousness and storms in as an infinite blast of overpowering nectar". We shouldn't limit truth to mere interplay of words; Truth must remain as is and truth must be seen in first person; Age-old fear, hunger and wounds all drop in a glance of the divinity. Yes, if you ask in a nutshell how truth is: It is "Brahman Satya Jagat Mithya"; There is only one truth; Atman the one Self of All alone is eternally existent, and all else derive their existence from That. हरे कृष्ण हरे कृष्ण कृष्ण कृष्ण हरे हरे हरे राम हरे राम राम राम हरे हरे॥

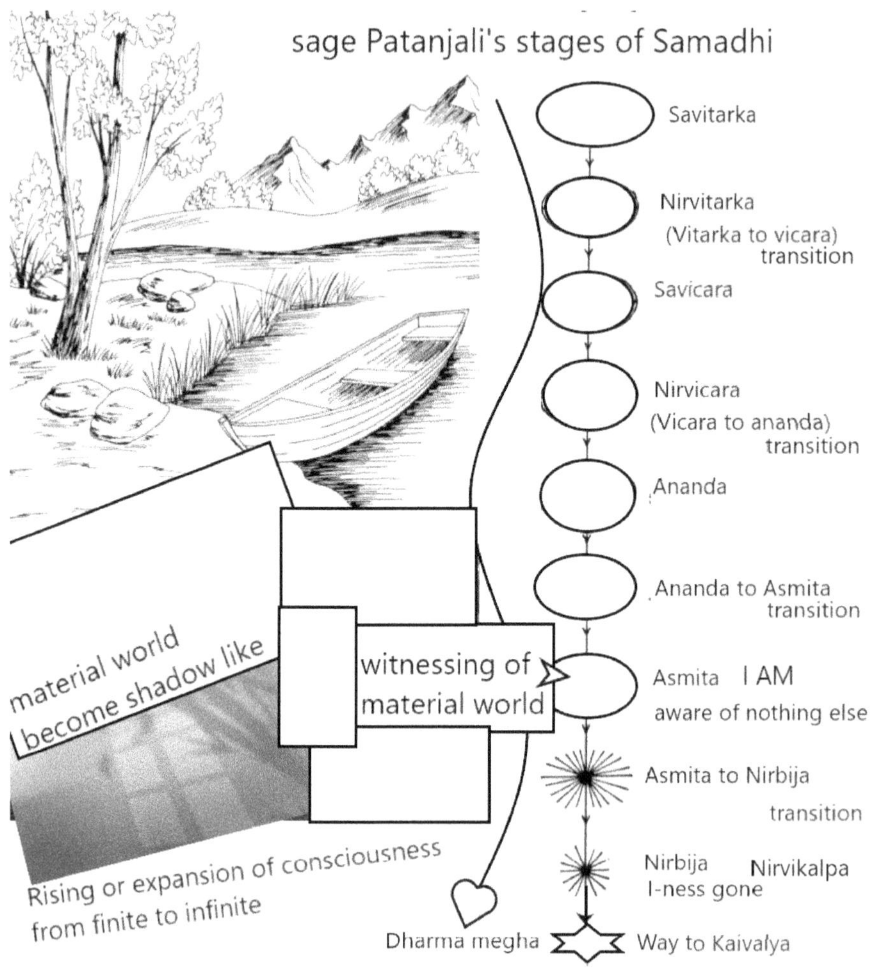

The 8th dhyana of buddhism too signals nirvikalpa.

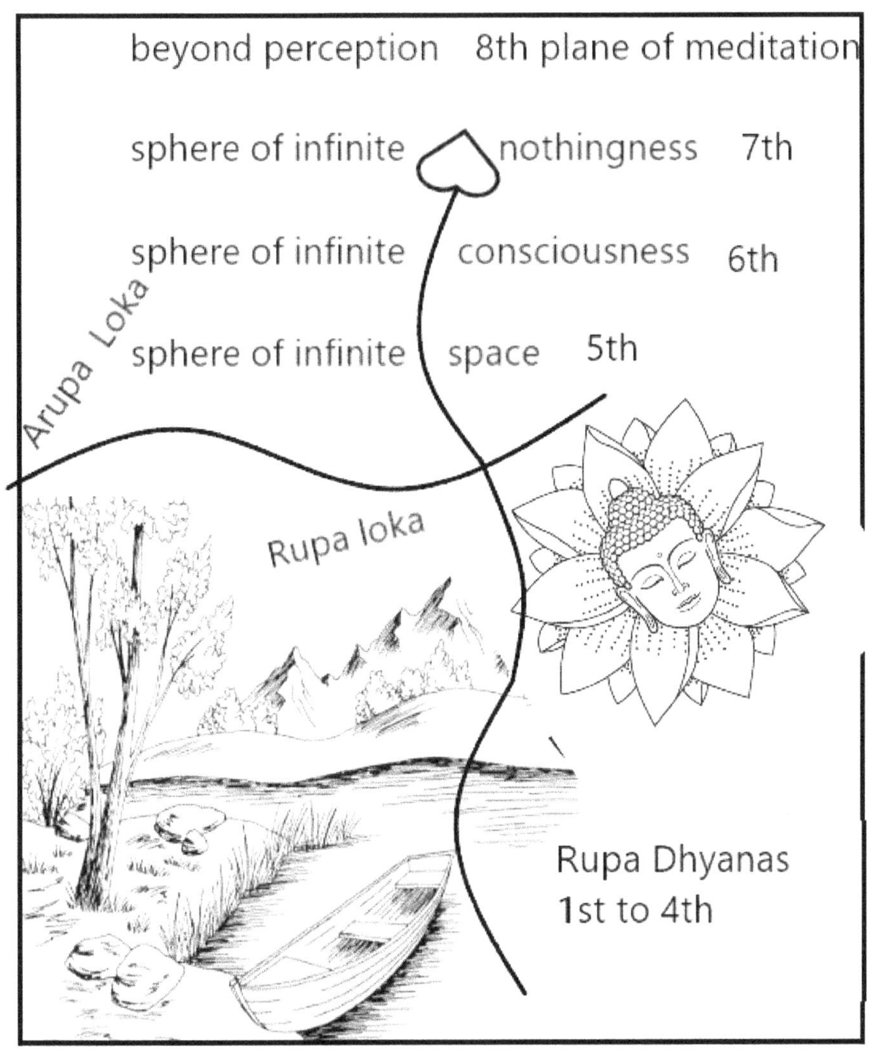

What is Sasmita samadhi of Patanjali? A magnificent stage comes, when ground is so fertile that no seed (thing) remains without immediately sprouting into consciousness, and whole cosmos melts and expands into one unified field of consciousness with terrible speed; Thou art That I am; Conversely, giving birth to infinite space (a little more condensed) with each descend; With further condensation, bubbles up the material universes with their myriad condensed (contracted) creatures. Samadhi is the tremendously unified consciousness followed by a lifting up of cosmos during descent. Seeker can experience this buoyancy like force. With each descent shadows are refilled with illusive substances.

asato ma sadgamaya

means, "Lead me from the asat to the sat."

tamaso ma jyotirgamaya

means "Lead me from darkness to light".

Merger: A few years pass in wonder as it merges with truth. Conscious mind merges first; subconscious merges next. Withdrawal is stronger and stronger as truth comes nearer and nearer.

What love with appearances?

What attachment to dream?

What attachment to lifeless images?

What expectation from lifeless things?

Is there any one behind an image we hanker to unite across lives?

Is there really any one behind an image we hanker for appreciation?

Is there anyone inside an image who we die to connect with?

And merging with Atman goes deeper and deeper;

And mind too turns drisya and fades.

A series of extra sensorial experiences presented hoping these rare snaps can convey the ecstatic moods and emotions one undergoes in trance. Who has word to describe the indescribable?

How does one attain Nirvikalpa Samadhi? The entry in nirvikalpa is beautifully put in this classic poem. The Infinitely conscious falls externally unconscious, finally dropping itself. One is beyond subject, object, and perception dipped in nectar.

Nirvikalpa:

Nirvikalpa Samadhi from **Swami Vivekananda**

Lo! The sun is not, nor the comely moon,

All light extinct; in the great void of space

Floats shadow-like the image-universe.

In the void of mind involute, there floats

The fleeting universe, rises and floats,

Sinks again, ceaseless, in the current "I".

Slowly, slowly, the shadow-multitude

Entered the primal womb, and flowed ceaseless,

The only current, the "I am", "I am".

Lo! 'Tis stopped, ev'n that current flows no more,

Void merged into void — beyond speech and mind!

Whose heart understands, he verily does.

One important Samadhi is remaining drunk and still transacting with the external world; The state of consciousness is "I am the whole; The dream like cosmos flows in me thrilling me, touching me; I am seeing infinite space; Like a drunken man on road, I am seeing things disappearing for a while as I go out of sense, and again seeing things appearing as I return to sense; I am in control of my little shadow (body)". The switch among these superposed threads of consciousness both finite and infinite is so swift that one can walk while remaining half sub merged in cosmic fog. All rise and fall in Me; Ages after, mind is seen in action behind all phenomena physical or mental.

In me rises desire,
In desire rises fire,
In fire rises forms,
Forms entangle awhile,
Forms talk, dance, and disappear.

Ages after in tear,
In me rises the desire for liberation,
That desire burns this desire,
And I expand back as purusha,
Whole prakriti dancing in Me.

I AM:

I am beyond; I am joy absolute;
I am impeccable; I am Atman.
When I am there, I am not here;
When I am here, I am not there.
When I am neither here nor there, I am omnipresent infinite space.
When I am not infinite space, I am back as I am;
I am infinite consciousness.

Sight of the Atman: Samadhi is the anti-climax for ego's uncontrolled dream for material conquest! No material height ever satiated the hunger of ego. But just one glance of the Atman changes ego's stand for ever. It waits eagerly for its own dissolution! In fact, it aids to destroy itself. Senses bring food but, the beggar ego is lost elsewhere. Nothing breaks its silence. It laments. Mind dances its best dance to no effect. The recoil is on. The snake no longer hisses. The charmer Atman has dealt the lethal blow without a word. Samadhi days are the sweetest stays in the material worlds when darkness and light are in deep embrace. There is no fight, no opposition, only surrender. **Only Samadhi insulates Jiva from death.** The very land of death and chaos turns the inner land of ecstasy and love.

The fort falls,
Just a glance all resistance gone,
Ego nowhere neither here nor there.
Ego and mind both die in ecstasy,
World slips away,
The background overshadows the foreground.
I am That.
Roams in valleys of mind relishing Samsara,
All look promising, time passes unnoticed,
All turn poison one day, heart burns, doubt rises, search begins.
Ages after recollects nectar looking poison,
Maya lifts, sees no poison anywhere, sees purusha ever united with prakriti!
What are the different types of Samadhi?
Nirvikalpa and Savikalpa are the main ones.
How does Samadhi come?
Ages of struggle after,
As deluded consciousness wakes up from deep slumber,
He sees his tiny body floating in his giant expansion,
He sees himself as the oneself of all,
He sees himself as infinite consciousness racing in infinite space,
He sees cosmos as an appearance swimming inside him.
He sees cosmos silent and playing like an innocent child,
All ferocity and noise gone,
All grave silence all his expansion,
He is the motion, he is the life in all,
He sees no one else apart from himself,

He sees shadows engaged with shadows,
He sees empty battlefields where his shadow fought for ages,
He sees not a single warrior left,
Where did they go?
He sees not a single drop of blood on the illusive swords,
All shadows, all illusions,
He alone fashioned this creation,
He alone is Maya, he alone is Prakriti,
He alone is Eshwar, he alone is killer, he alone is killed,
Millions of cosmoses come and go in his mind, yet he is detached.
His shadow no longer asks, "Who he is and where others went?".
Om! Om! Om!

"Mind sparkles over body; Consciousness sparkles over mind; One goes beyond all". The first spark lands one in mind, while the second takes one beyond mind. Millions of births after when the stone finally speaks, it takes years or even births to close eyes in awe. The constant flood of revelations fills seeker with wonder and ecstasy. The seeker is pulled afar to the eternal fount head of joy. Samadhi routinely visits.

Acting ends:
Eternal monsoon of consciousness strikes.
Conscious drowns; Subconscious follows.
Outer curtain (external senses) falls; Inner curtain rises.
Real show (heavens) unfolds, World a deep dream.
Little joys it hankered after go unlimited, unending.
Eternal overwhelms love-lorn; Little actor(ego) lost in his lap!

Once gross is seen as dream ecstasy begins. Slowly ecstasy deepens and intoxication swipes away even the mind. One lands in Nirvikalpa. **Ecstasy devours gross;** All dream; Ecstasy devours mind too.

In penance all solids, liquids, gases of all universes turn cosmic fluid, and the master magician rises from background. World turns a vast ocean of intuition where floats sun, moon, earth, and stars. Ekam Evadvitiyam Brahma.

Veil lifts. The little desire still left projects some dolls for the slender ego. Separation from Samsara nears. Sun sets in Self. The veiler, veiling and veiled all turn one.

"What is that? What is that?" Jiva wonders,

Oh, that is the substratum in which this wonderful world is woven!
Oh, that is the magical substance behind roopa, rasa etc.
Oh, I was in dream screaming and laughing unaware!

Wonder strikes:

When the wonder strikes, the seeker is awestruck drowning in its real Self.

Conscious drowns,
Subconscious drowns,
Memory fades,
What dream? What awake? What deep sleep?
I the infinite consciousness alone am, flooding my Jagat,

Can there be poverty in a magical creation? Millions of earths can be created at will in a moment. Poverty is deliberate to trigger desire and competition. To chase the mirage is the magical play created by the creator.

What you see:

What you see is mind, where you see is mind,
what you hear is mind, what you touch is mind,
What you smell is mind, what you taste is mind.
Whole cosmos seen rising and setting in mind.
All doubts dispelled; the seer of mind is you.

Who doesn't seek evergreen youth?

Who doesn't seek unbroken love?
But all this possible only in movie.
In dream too fear hunts,
In dream too we fall,
In dream too we are not fully free,
Such is our load,
Such is our mental conditions.
As you meet the loveliest companion,
Body no more grows old,
Mind no more feels loneliness,
Disease no more hunts nest after nest,
Fear no more holds back dream,
Soars the intuition engulfing jagat.
Eternal youth returns,
Eternal love returns,

Bliss feeds on bliss.

What is Mukti?

Seeing own's real Self as the orchestrator of Maya which is behind the infinite wheel of cause and effect, one escapes from the clutch of causation. There is no other way!

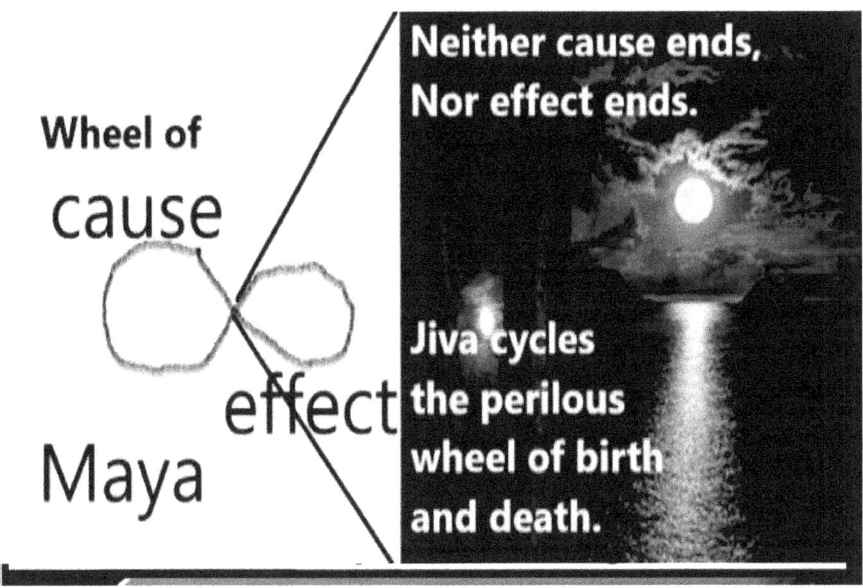

Who is behind the creation? Through power of maya, He expands into Maya and Eshwar. Ego is created fed by ignorance of Maya, Eshwar and Atman.

He is he; He is she,

He is beyond he and she.

He finally sees whole nature back as ecstasy.

The part expands as whole.

Over window of mind, space flows in and out with shadows multitude.

How do you feel when you see truth? For the first time you see the beauty of Samsara in its full glory. Cosmos turns thousand times more beautiful. You missed it in fear! You are even reluctant to leave as spells cast by maya temporarily returns. Such is the beauty of this magical creation in its fully bloomed states (heavens). However, nectar overshadows all and fully inebriated ego leaves. **Projection of Jagat** by mind ends for ever.

Astral travel begins,

You outgrow cosmos, cosmos in grows.

You stand stationary in solitude,

Cosmos the dream progresses in you.

Your little old body swims in you.

When my beloved comes,

Fluid of intuition becomes food, his lap my bed,

Clock hides, space hides.

Living a while among the shadows the seeker departs for ever. Things no more look real. Pull of things vanishes. The invincible looking desire recoils with nothing to feed on.

All shadows,

Shadow sun, shadow moon, shadow cities, shadow hills, all shadows.

Shadows playing among shadows, shadows turn the whole creation.

Who remains to desire?

What is left to desire?

How long can one stay among shadows?

It departs.

Brahman Satya Jagat Mithya.

Alone I come, alone I go, Alone I am.

Of what use their (egos) fights?

Over what they fight? Of what use their pining?

The faraway bodies too are my shadows,

I alone am the life in all giant and small.

World a beautiful cave flowing in you,

Solitary timeless spaceless existence.

Life flows back, all in rhythm.

Peace abounds, joy abounds, journey complete.

You infinitely spread, sun shining in your lap.

You still descend at times,

A little sleep, a little food needed to keep this soul alive.

Home comes closer its fragrance blinding,

Sleep stops, feeding stops, mind beyond,

You wide awake ever blissful and serene.

Wait ends, dawn comes, bell rings, door opens, darshan at last!

The golden moment arrives.

Desolation deepens,

Road less travelled comes,

Little ahead road disappears.
All communication lost for ever,
Quiet flows the dawn.

Thunder strikes when least expected after prolonged dry spells. So, don't lose hope. He does come. Fall and rise, fall, and rise till the truth is revealed. Merger sensation if expressed in words "Invisible limbs spread to infinity". Another eye (if we so call it) gets superposed over this eye. One lands in an alien land of joy unlimited.

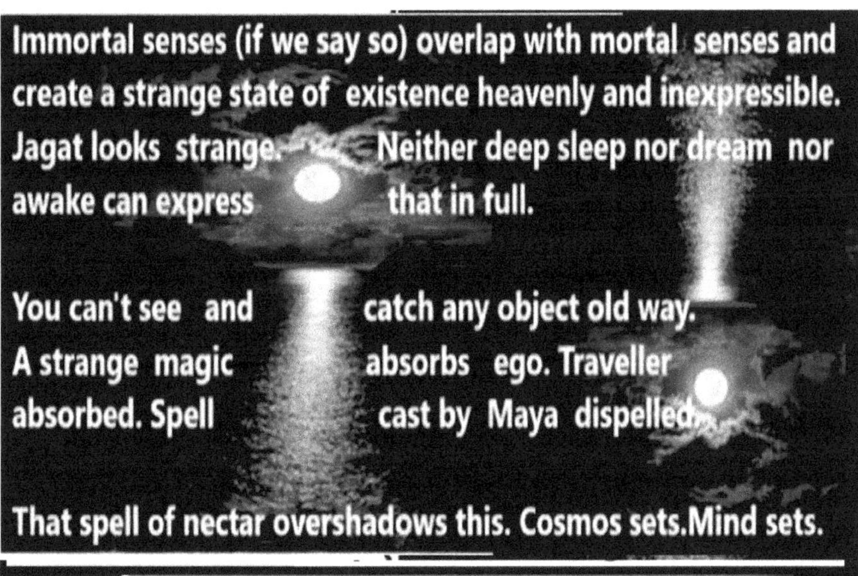

The habit of chasing shadows comes to an end.

Time and again we run after shadows, forgetting that neither we nor the objects we run after exist as they look.

Wall falls:
Millions of years later, passes the storm of liberation ego in centre,
Earth meets sky, all fly in wind,
Spell cast for ages ends,
Falls the walls of pain.

The sign of upcoming Samadhi is clear right from childhood. Mind is constantly pulled afar from material engagements without any immediate reason. One is unaware what pulls mind away and where. Abnormal tides of joy assail the shores mind, pulling into rapture. Nature sings deep, calls deep, connects deep.

Practice: Just as we regularly clean house, so too we must consistently disinfect mind by japa (prayer), tapa(penance), asana, pranayama, satsang, self-sacrifice, self-surrender, kshama (pardon others), self-less love, service to needy, detached work, reflection on four-fold sufferings. What we value the most is our love. Just as a miser's mind is always on money, so too a seeker's mind is ever on the path of freedom. With extreme love one prays.

Unaware we return again and again,
Same blunder repeats,
Engrossed in shows, lost in rainbow of emotions,

We miss the background.
In twilight hours left to lament, it's too late!
We still veiled, projection slows,
Periphery of thought gets closer,
Forced withdrawal begins, speech merges in mind,
Disregarding sighs, sobs and tear prana snatched away,
Wheel rolls on where nobody knows.

We come again and again but forgets in pain of death and birth. We start very late and miss the bus. We keep trying unaware till eternal dawn flows.

When you hear whispers of inanimate,
when you hear whispers of meadows,
when mind has shed all gross,
when feeling has gone extremely sublime,
when minute ripples of mind seen,
when all serene under tranquil sky,
when all noise inner and outer absorbed,
when intuition soars higher and higher,
when you are in extra sensorial,
when you are back in harmony with you,
when little centre has touched infinite,
when ego weaves garland of surrender,
when ego eager to embrace eternal,
when ego absorbed by divine rapture,
when body forgotten in ecstasy of union,
when you see all cosmos entering you,
when nothing remains to be owned,
when nothing remains separated from you,
then know golden hour is close, and ego
getting washed away in Brahmajyoti,
then know Krishna is close,
then know cosmos slipping away for ever,
then know liberation has finally dawned!!!

Ego is absorbed in truth as mind dances with the carrot (thing that amuses mind and senses).

Magic is ever on in this infinite theatre of maya! But, we are lost elsewhere missing the magical spells birth after birth.   We are divorced from nature; Not only that, we are insensitive and rude to it due to our excessive greed and preoccupation with name and fame. We have forgotten our basic lessons of life: Living in rhythm with both external and internal nature.

Align lifestyle with nature.

A beautiful note of magic, a shy moon briskly walking away through clouds, fragrance of a little forest flower with murmering bees hovering   around, a faraway hill inviting the tired sun for a rest, view of a snowclad mountain in the pristine hour of dawn, view of a cowherd boy returning among   his herd in dusk, view of sun gently rising above the horizon pushing the   stubborn clouds away etc.   all can connect and trasport us to our sublime state.

A cave is as noisy as the mind.

In fact, anything that overwhelms mind can trigger samadhi. A beautiful quote from W. H. Davies reminds us of our burdened mind.

What is this life if, full of care,
We have no time to stand and stare.

Be kind. A little care for somebody in need invites his love. He sees.

Ascent:
As Jiva ascends to wonderland of consciousness,
As Jiva is devouring all identities it asks:
What is this happening to me? Where did I reach?
This is neither dream land nor physical, where am I?
It is not same Jagat I roamed before! How I float without water?
Where is north? Where is south? Where is where? Where is there?
You walk inside you;
your tiny body and its surroundings swim inside you.

Absorption

'I' sees the spectacular sight in infinite space:

It sees "its tiny shadow like body and surrounding around it" navigating inside it through the tunnel of seses, just as a glow worm sparkling and swimming in air in the depth of night.

The physical road we travel on, exactly look like the trail of a glow worm in night. All cosmos races into it for its existence. Whose death O dear! Can't believe?

Progress of Samadhi: "With what speed it expands difficult to tell; This inside, that inside, all devoured within; All engulfing consciousness swallowing giant bodies in no time, still expanding; Like a massive and sudden flood submerging the sand beds with infinite speed; The racing of consciousness is exquisite!

Wonder is, wherever eye extends, all territories seen flowing within; No noise, no resistance; Skies, clouds, moons, suns all gently touched by all expanding consciousness; The mystical eyes are pulled into deep space, a wonderful sleepiness accompanies as the pull progresses; An exquisite state of consciousness". This is the infinite pull of Samadhi as ego expands infinitely submerging whole cosmos within. Atman disarms ego in just one glance and surprisingly, ego aids its own destruction inebriated!

How does one descend from Samadhi?

Through the bridge of remaining desire, one returns to land of death as a different person. Body is same but, there is sea change in perception, all perceived in the light of Atman. The kala is transcended at last!!

How does ego spend the remaining days?

We all know, when night approaches and mother comes calling, how the child is reluctant to leave its much-adored sand houses. The ego looks back at this earth. In fear of death, it never saw the beauty and depth of the creation in full. Now that the fear is gone, it looks wonderstruck at the same fort again, at the same doors again and recalls its struggle for morsels of food thrown at it from outside; All was in fact coming from within. It senses that, it is the king of kings paraded and arrested in his own kingdom for stealing morsels of food. It all happened by the mighty forces of Maya. What looked so impregnable and far is but an illusion.

Fort open, cage open, shackles removed,

Freedom long awaited beckons,

Wind of liberation heals the wounds.

A sweet wave hitherto unknown assails the shores of mind,

A few more moments in her worlds, cosmos sets within, eternal is back!

What is Mahasamadhi?

When all prarabdha karma is settled, and no more desire remains, the remaining ego has no chance to take rebirth. One attains Mahaparinirvana or body is released in Nirvikalpa Samadhi.

How long this hanging out as a bunch of thoughts?
His call irresistible O Jada senses (Jagat)!
Lets part ways O mind, enough of dance, our journey was thus far!
My boat has come, my Atman beckons O mind, I have to leave!

I can't swim back in your river O mind, I am dipped in his ocean!
Pitted against your banks of sorrows I am worn out.

As I fall here from there, I am torn into pieces (distractions) and cry;
As I embrace Him I soar again; He has absorbed me from within.

Let senses feed you the last morsels (last life) O mind!
His hangover, His fragrance is enough for Me; I am absorbed;
I am in his Garbhagriha (idol room in temple); We are reconnected.

Its no tale O mind, Its my truth, its your truth, its the truth of all!
We now meet beyond time and space!

In arrogance I missed Him, in humility I see Him, in love I get Him.
My boat has come, my Atman beckons O mind, I have to leave!

Wait becomes unbearable:

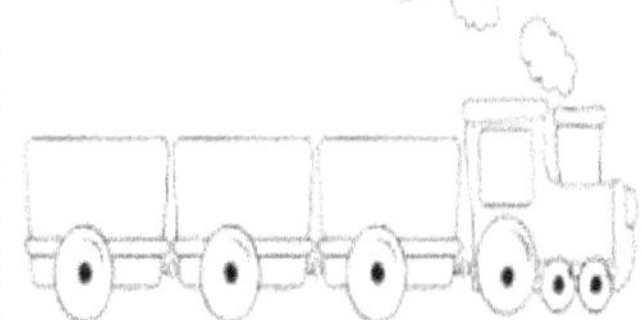

Mahasamadhi: Samadhi continues burning the conscious mind. All the entanglements however little are settled, and the seeker withdraws more and more from the mundane world. Intoxicated seeker dances in inner solitude ecstatic of union. As long as traces of both conscious and subconscious hunger in mind remains, the expanded (I am the whole) contracts (I am this little body) to transact. Complete unbinding of I from this body and whole world begins when dream or subconscious ripples too stops, as there is no hidden hunger left to be satiated. The awake state is flooded (Samadhi) throughout the day so much so that, the little i slips into only the dream as a hideout (like a tiger in hideout to eat the gathered flesh). Then, Samadhi ripens and continues for hours as the expanded I rewinds back to the oldest seeds (far older births) and slip away from there to eternity or Mahasamadhi comes. The whole forest and all seeds are burnt as millions of thunders finish the avidya completely. How can you talk to shadows? In his light senses can't catch anything. World turns a dream. Departing time nears.

Periphery is truth:
The little hunger wanes, senses grow feebler,
No more hiss, no more movements,
Inner bell rings louder, circumference grows infinite,
Periphery leaves centre, truth alone is.

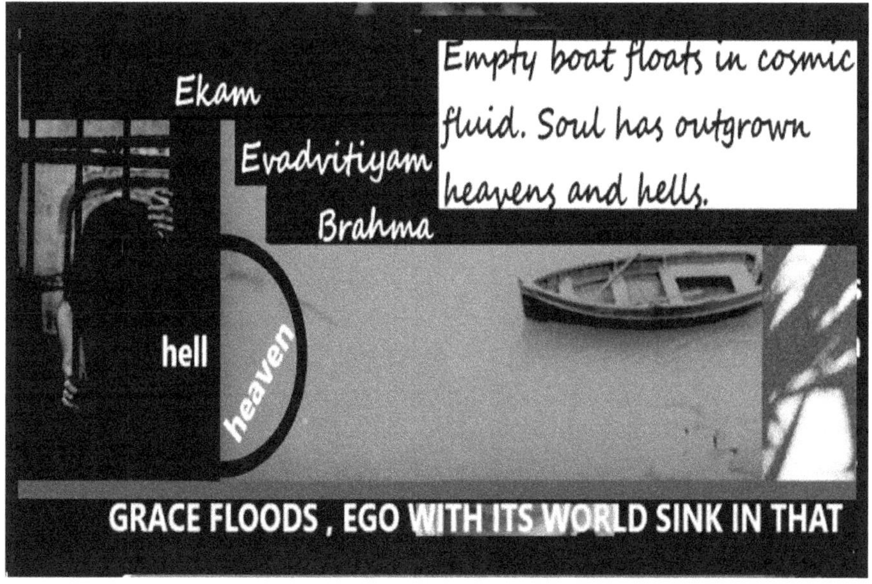

The Way Ahead

Let us remember the main point of this book: Eternal solution to life's myriad problems is not a myth, but a fact. Whole book is a record of a successful search shared for posterity. Nectrine Atman alone is, and all else borrow their existence from that one Self of all the Atman, and by Yoga we can meet truth in this very life if we are genuine. Solutions to the sufferings lie in the sufferings alone. Effort, surrender and prayer to the unknown invites grace. Faith gradually develops if we keep on reflecting, if we keep on trying, if we keep on praying. Satsang is the way to eternal light. You are immortal to the core.

One more important point which immediately works: Body must be conditioned by taking simple, light, and satvic food along with right sleep, light excercise, light asana, and light pranayama. We must adjust inputs within our body limit, neither more, nor less. Without that progress in sadhana is slow. What is the use of lamenting in very old age when even normal sitting becomes tough. Make hay while the sun shines. Like a wood pecker we must keep meditating; Like an ant we must prepare for the rainy day which can come any time.

Here's a little recap of what we covered: We primarily touched on several intriguing questions of our existence specifically "Who we are? Who reincarnates? Whether God exists? Whether karma decides our fate? Is there a solution to our problems? Is the world purposeless? Do heavens and hells exist and if so, then where?". These questions impelled me to seek truth. I am sure they have either reached you or about to run riots in you. They are natural to come and are the signs of the journey to eternal existence. No need to nip these doubts in the bud as useless efforts, they are the signs of blooming of divinity in you.

Then, what's next? The sufferings of this world are not new to us. Many have faced the daunting challenges and come out victorious. If you have a little courage please go through the below paragraph about me just to apprise you of the pathetic state of affairs that I had been mercilesly thrown into, not very far back.

Once I was terribly depressed. I still remember how I used to walk like a corpse in deep anguish and frustration, not for a day, not for a month, but for a decade; I was challenged in my own den. I am sure a fraction of that pain would have bent the spines of the most courageous ones; I recollect how I hided my face from others thinking "What others would think of me? I am a failure. I am fallen. I am a loser. I am thrown away to languish in cold, with no means to defend myself; I am lost in the mad race for money; I am rejected; I am dumped in garbage. Who would understand me? Who would take my pain? Who on this earth has patience and courage I could pour out my mind to? This world is behind woman and gold, this world is after glitters. Who would listen to this fragile and shipwrecked soul? Why whatever branches I try to hold for a little solace breaks down. Where am I heading to? Where are others and where I am? Its of no use to attempt to catch others; My bus was missed long, and its of no use lamenting over split milk. My youth has waned, my sight has come down. Is there a way out? Why are there so much sufferings? How can I face the world again. How can I get back the lost rhthm in life, how can I reconnect and dance again with nature? O unknown help me! Neither my hunger went, nor my hope survived the scare of fate. I am rejected by the same society which I had rejected in my early college days. Where went the tall hopes, where went the achievements, where went the romantic days? Where what went wrong when and why? Only a faint hope of eternal life kept this Jiva walking on the streets of this matrial world.

And the monsoon of liberation started when least expected; Realization dawned when all hopes had long departed!! **So what's next?** Yes, if you stick to meditation with determination and a little courage, life changes for ever. Eternal hope returns; Age-old thirst gets satiated for ever.One becomes complete; We only have the key to the solution to life's problems; We are immortal and situations can't break us; We are beyond; Our efforts are cumulative over births whether you believe or not. How often we repent for returning from the door of victory? My best wishes for all your future endeavours, be it material or, immaterial. All your tiny steps now are the foundations of your giant steps ahead. In unequivocal terms I affirm that, life blooms to perfection as we help ourselves by treading the path of Yoga with an iron mind. We are here to win the race of life. Our engagement doesn't end here. We are eternally connected. I feel you. Yes, we can stay connected and make life successful. We can exchange our thoughts in many of my social sites whose links are shared below.

Nothing heals like hope, nothing connects like hope.
If we meditate, life is bound to take a turn for the better.

When result of play clear, can any brief upset bother audience?
Our problems are mental, physical but a tip of the ice.
Physical ailments are tough, but mental far tougher,
When mental heals, physical is bearable.

Many things came and went, what stayed with us?
This phase of life too would pass away, all transient all illusive.
Lets meditate proper, lets face sufferings, lets exploit sufferings to end sufferings.
Lets see what divine messages are hidden in it, let this birth ushers in hope eternal.

He sends his messenger again and again, but who on earth is awake to see?
All busy building up egos, even those on path of spiritualty!
Their love knee deep, their compassion a farce!

Like Duryodhana they don't like truth, yet they say they are helpless before mind.
They can't budge an inch, yet they say solution is not in their hand.

They smear the beautiful creation with blood, yet they preach universal peace.
They preach others, instead they should preach themselves.

Truth is but a step away, yet they make a show of their knowledge.
Path to eternity costs nothing, yet they blame fate!
Love costs nothing, hate costs everything. Yet they love hate pretending love.

A simple life, a little air and a little prayer, who on earth can't afford?
We are in a wrong boat, and worse still we are aware!

We (ego) refuse to go, we ignore vivek, we pretend, yet we say 'Its fate'.
Ego is the liar; Ego is the villain; Ego is the evil; Ego is the blocker to its real Self.

A rare one somewhere cries aloud and he is picked up, he is on patrol everywhere!

When he graces, all laws reverse, all learnings reverse, all things go nothing.
Here absolute power corrupts absolutely, there, eternal hope heals eternally.

Lets try sincerly for univerasal brotherhood and love. We are all entangled at universal level. We can't escape karma which is at a cosmic level. The internal fabric of this creation is but one, and any ups somewhere is bound to pull somewhere something down. We see little, yet we make noise.

Let good sense prevail, let love bloom, let eternal hope dispels all gloom from the face of earth! Let all smile. Let us meditate, let us surrender to his will, let us take a fresh look at our problems as well at the problems faced by whole mankind. We are one and forever connected. This world is a live dream. Best of luck for whereever you intend to be! Bye!